Highly
Irregular

The
Newspaper Columns of
Carl Bode

SOUTHERN ILLINOIS UNIVERSITY PRESS
Carbondale and Edwardsville

Feffer & Simons, Inc.
London and Amsterdam

Library of Congress Cataloging in Publication Data

Bode, Carl, 1911–
  Highly irregular.

  I. Title.
PS3503.0164H5   814'.5'4   74–8704
ISBN 0–8093–0684–0

To John Anderson
of the Washington *Post*
who started me on my downward way, and
Bradford Jacobs
of the Baltimore *Evening Sun*
who greased the slope

Contents

Precede

(Preface, that is)

The prescription I propose: take one at a time. The point is that these columns were written at intervals and published at intervals. Even the classical columnists, Addison and Steele, are best read that way. Faced with a fat volume of their *Spectator* essays you can't help feeling a bit daunted; if you pause between essays, as did Addison and Steele themselves, you come out just right. On the other hand, if, kindled by my columns, you read with feverish eagerness straight through them all, I'll be the last to object.

What I've done is to select for this book from the columns which have appeared in the Washington *Post* and the Baltimore *Evening Sun*. The approach of both my editors, John Anderson first and then Brad Jacobs, was civilized indeed. They told me to write when I felt like it and it turned out that I felt like it on the average of once every three weeks, maybe when the moon was right. The fact that I could write without a deadline and with no constraints but my own made it all the more fun. No splendid misery here.

Naturally many of the columns bear the print of a definite time and place, and sometimes of a particular occasion. In their background there's a mixed bag of facts: that I teach American literature at the University of Maryland in College Park; that I divide much of my off-campus time between Washington and Baltimore; that both as a writer and a teacher I'm attracted by two dizzyingly different literary rebels, Henry David Thoreau and H. L. Mencken; that I'm delighted by my students and bemused by their ways; and that I'm fascinated by the popular culture of our time as it shifts or sashays around.

A few times I've put in an afternote for the reader's convenience. For example, I've noted for "A Walk in the Wonderful Sun" that I've kept the observations, made three years after the famous March on Washington of August 28, 1963, intact and unrevised because I thought they might have a mild historical interest. But ordinarily I've let the columns speak for themselves. They sometimes betray the fact that times change, but you and I already know that.

The titles I thought up for these columns have been restored. At the papers they got not titles but headlines and so I've put back the titles I started with. Then too I've done revision of the text here and there, in places where I thought I could improve the expression.

My grateful acknowledgment for permission to reprint goes to the *Evening Sun*, where the bulk of these columns first appeared; and to the Washington *Post* for all of the remainder except "H. L. Mencken, Come Back," first printed in the New York *Times*, and "Greatness at a Glance," first printed in the Washington *Star-News*. To those two papers I'm grateful as well.

Carl Bode

Hyattsville, Maryland
April 1, 1974

1

Sealing It with Sex

"Men Act; Women Talk." Who said it? John Wayne? William Buckley? Black Angus? Or "Words are Women; Deeds are Men." Or "Manly Deeds; Womanly Words." Who said it?

The answer is: the whole state of Maryland, and for more than 300 years.

It's the motto on the Maryland State Seal. A hundred thousand copies must be floating around the state, from Frostburg to Frederick, from Girdletree to Leitersburg. They're stamped on the state stationery; and you can imagine the streams of correspondence flowing from Annapolis and Baltimore, as well as the more minor seats of state government. They're chiseled into the stone of state buildings. They ripple on the multitudinous state flags. I'm amazed that the motto didn't trigger a furious feminist revolt decades ago. But all that has happened so far is a few calls for its removal from several of our women legislators in the State Assembly. The chief reason it's slid by up to now is that it's in Italian, *Fatti Maschi, Parole Femine.* Surely that shouldn't have been sufficient to save it, though.

Anyhow it fascinates me and so I've done a bit of digging into its history. To go back to the beginning, I found that we know little about the first form of the seal because it was stolen in 1644 and no picture of it remains. But we know that the seal devised after that one is substantially the seal we see today. Its reverse side (the side the state uses) showed the coat of arms of Lord Baltimore. The arms were quartered, as they say, for the Calvert family and for the Crossland family as well, from whom Lord Baltimore was descended on his mother's side.

To anyone who believes as I do in the mystery of words, the official description of the arms is a delight. For the Calverts: "a paly of six pieces or and sable, a bend counter-changed." For the Crosslands: "quarterly argent and gules, a cross bottony counter-changed."

Supporting the arms on either side are a fancily dressed farmer and a fisherman, one standing with a spade and the other holding a limp mackerel. The fisherman, incidentally, may represent not Chesapeake Bay but Lord Baltimore's other domain in New-foundland, then called Avalon.

In that form the seal sailed along for better than a century. Then came the Revolution, American that is, and the Assembly ordered the seal altered. Out went feudalism and romance, look-ing sadly over their shoulder. In came democracy, spitting on its hands and getting down to business. Unfortunately its artistic efforts left something to be desired. In fact the new seal was a big yawn. It featured a tobacco barrel, with leaf tobacco lying on top. Next to it stood a couple of sheaves of wheat and behind it sailed a ship. And the motto? "Industry the Means and Plenty the Re-sult." Pure porridge!

Even Maryland, already famed for toleration, couldn't stand such a seal. From time to time minor modifications were quietly made. In 1854 came a major one. The Calverts marched back on the seal, with their quartered arms and farmer and fisherman. But "Manly Deeds; Womanly Words" didn't make it; the old motto was left out. My guess is that some local Elizabeth Cady Stanton said grimly, "Now look, boys . . ." and the legislators looked. However, from today's point of view they didn't do much better. The motto they substituted was *Crescite et Multiplicamini*. In this era of Zero Population Growth who needs the injunction "Increase and Multiply"?

Still, it was an improvement over "Manly Deeds." Neverthe-less in 1876, somehow or other, the old motto slid back in. The ancient arms of Maryland were finally restored to their integrity, as one nineteenth-century sexist said. That integrity has managed to survive till now.

Not that there haven't been mealymouthed efforts at appeasement. Once or twice Chesapeake diplomats have hinted that the motto really means "Courage and Courtesy." Nonsense. We know what it means. It's a put-down, a put-down of women. So in common fairness it's got to go.

But what should we insert in its place? Surely not "Industry the Means and Plenty the Result." Surely not "Increase and Multiply." It's hard to select the right motto. I realize what the motto should do, however. It should inform us; it should embody a truth of experience; and it should be timely ("relevant" used to be the term) in both substance and style.

With eyes modestly directed at the ground, I myself have a motto to offer Maryland. It's the fruit of years of observation of Maryland life. It is in fact one of the axioms which I've termed Bode's Laws. There are five of them and they cover the whole subject of human life. The Third Law is the one I'm willing to donate to the state of Maryland. And it tells it like it is: "Error Crushed to the Earth Will Rise Again." I believe it would look pretty under the Baltimore arms.

2

Britannica Revisited

I was brought up to believe in the eleventh edition. I was told—I don't even remember when—that the later editions were jazzed up by Sears Roebuck after Sears, of all organizations, bought the *Britannica.* I was also told that the flashy new information was provided by the same salesmen who dashed off the descriptions of merchandise in the catalog. But the eleventh edition had been graved on tablets of stone, by learned men with lined faces who labored late at the British Museum to make the tiniest word accurate.

Now I have a couple of the hallowed volumes open before me, Volume 7, *Con to Dem,* and Volume 23, *Ref to Sai.* They bring back a throng of boyhood recollections. Among them the fact that I never learned to make a beeline to the thing I wished to look up. Lured by earlier entries, I stopped often on the way. Perhaps I intended to check "Cromwell, Oliver" in Volume 7 for a theme topic. "Constellation," for instance, could easily waylay me. Doubtless I stared eagerly at the stellar diagrams but failed, as I always did, to see a lady in the constellation Cassiopoeia, just as I failed to see the Man in the Moon. "Look," my elders would urge me impatiently, "there's his nose and there are his eyes." All I could see was a scrambled egg. Then there was "Costume," lavishly illustrated. "Henry, Prince of Wales, and Occleve the Poet" says one caption. In the illustration both men are robed; Henry stands while Occleve kneels. Royalty, eyes glazed, looks down as usual on Literature. I finally reached the Cromwell entry but, as the travel posters suggest, getting there was half the fun.

Volume 23, *Ref to Sai*, is richer still. For one thing it has more royalty than ever, and kings and queens and their offspring have always fascinated me. I note an entry on Robert, oldest son of William the Conqueror. The *Britannica*, invariably tactful to the hilt, observes that Robert had several "natural children." For years I wondered what other kind of children there were. Unnatural ones? Then there is an entry on Roman art, with abundant plates. I looked at the photos of the portrait busts: handsome, high-coiffed women and hardmouthed men. Then back to royalty under the heading of "Round Table," for some information on my favorite ruler King Arthur. I learned that he devised the Round Table because of a fight among his warriors, one Yuletide Day, about who should have the best seat at the old long table. I also learned that Arthur punished the warrior who had begun the fight by slaying all his male kinfolk and "cutting off the noses of his women-folk." My hero!

But I'd better be candid. What really pulled me to Volume 23 was the entry "Reproductive System," for I recall how avidly and often I scanned that one as a boy. The first time came right after a knowing youth on my block described the act of intercourse to me. I still recall my unbelieving blurt, "You must be kidding," and my retreat at a run to Volume 23. But the article was wrapped in Latin, with words like *vulva* to befuddle me, so I wasn't much the wiser.

That was one trouble with the *Britannica*. To understand a given subject, you had to have so much background information that you didn't really need to look up the subject in the first place. The authors of the entries always assumed that you knew all about, say, the Council of Trent, or dalmatics, or gnomonic projections. Many a time I groaned at the *Britannica*'s obscurity.

Today I apologize to the shades of the authors of the old *Britannica*, who still move at midnight in the moonlit British Museum. I apologize for my groans at their offhand references to the Council of Trent or dalmatics. For I've been trying to write the entry on Henry David Thoreau for the next edition of the *Britannica*, now escaped from the hot hand of Sears Roebuck and under the benign protection of what used to be called an eleemosynary institution. The effort is a trial of the spirit. Either you must cut away the most illuminating details and most instructive examples, or you end with twice the number of words the editors ordered. The net effect is that you are forced to develop a prose style so abstract, so bleak, that it could be dubbed Encyclopedese. You have room for two sentences of Encyclopedese on, for instance, Thoreau's early education and three on New England Transcendentalism. His education was important, as was of course his role in Transcendentalism. For years I've been examining Transcendentalism with mingled delight and exasperation, for I still don't understand it as well as I wish. How can I reduce my complicated confusions to three sentences?

To add insult to injury, as the poet says, the very editors who still make the authors write Encyclopedese now demand elegance from them also. I quote the exhortation by the chief editor: "Finally, there is the matter of style. Clarity, of course, is basic. We hope, in addition, for literary grace; perhaps even elegance."

Elegance, huh?

3

Faculty Fancies

I admit it. I love to play Newspaperman. The red press-card on the dashboard of my 1948 Hudson; the red ticket dangling from a button of my monkscloth jacket; the chance to pass through doors slammed shut to the public. All these allure me.

I also love to play Coach. This I haven't been able to do as much, so far at any rate. Some of my friends on my university's faculty are in physical education. I support them in favoring compulsory gym for all students, because I believe in doing good to people even when they resent it. Perhaps especially when they resent it. So I've been on my friends' side in the university senate when compulsory gym was being sniped at by weedy professors who vowed, as they wheezed into their cigarettes, that nobody would ever again be forced to do knee bends in Cole Field House. I've nobly advocated compulsory knee bends. Do my friends in physical education reward me with a jazzy coach's jacket, so I can wear it with my flannels and Adidas and be hailed, even if by mistake, as "Coach"? You know the answer, well aware as you are of the marble hardness of the human heart.

If by a happy chance I get to play both Newspaperman and Coach, I radiate satisfaction like a Franklin stove. And something like this has been happening for the past couple of weeks. Let me grab you by the elbow and tell you how.

A magazine commissioned me to do an article on Charles Grice Driesell, otherwise "Lefty," my university's plangently publicized basketball coach. What makes Lefty tick? the editor asked me. What's he really like? What does his curious renown tell us about our country? (This was shrewd on the editor's part; he knows that I relish answering the unanswerable.)

In the course of hustling materials for the article, I was invited to drive one evening with Lefty and Jim Maloney, his bright young assistant, to Charlottesville. They were going to scout the Virginia-Duke basketball game. We got there, marched through the crowd, and made for the press table where seats waited for us.

"If the guys on my old block could only see me now" I sighed, for the picture we made on entering must have been fantastic. We stalked in, single file. Lefty first, looking eight feet tall and wearing a fancy suede-cut suit; Jim third, wearing Coach's Conservative oxford gray; me in between, wearing a turtle-neck sweater and the purple elephant-leg levis I'd gotten for Christmas. Lefty was chewing gum. Jim was chewing gum. I hadn't chewed gum for ten years but I wasn't going to be outstripped. I was chewing gum. At the half I swaggered up to the president's box, where I'd glimpsed a good friend of mine and his wife. After greeting them I nonchalantly offered each a stick of Spearmint, hoping to set back Virginia gentility a full generation. They refused with thanks, explaining that they preferred plug tobacco to chicle. It was a great evening.

Another memorable night while I was doing "The Driesell Story" came a week later, at Cole Field House when Maryland itself played Virginia. Every one of the 14,000 seats had somebody in it; the joint jumped with adrenalin. Press tables ringed the entire floor—this game was national news. I wandered around on the floor before the game. I waved genially at colleagues in the stands who looked down at me with jaws dropping. I waved at the chancellor of my university, and I could see on his face the wild hope that I was abandoning teaching for sportswriting. Then I stopped in the press room to listen to the real reporters. Every now and then I held my end up by nodding sagely. Then the roar mounted, the teams ran in through the lanes of cheerleaders, and the game began.

By the end of the first half we knew that Maryland was due to win. The teams trotted to the locker rooms; the coaches, led by Lefty, trailed behind them. The members of the press headed for the typewriters and telephones—along with the free cokes and hot dogs—of the press room. While they phoned their first-hand stories to their papers, I phoned Ellen and asked what we were going to have for dinner the next day. I looked pretty professional, muttering into the mouthpiece as if I had a scoop.

When I strolled back to the press seats one of my students hailed me, "Mr. Bode, why did Lefty do all that subbing in the first half?"

"I'll tell you," I began wisely, and then the Maryland Pep Band drowned out the insight I was about to offer. It was just as well.

Still, this offered me an idea. Why not take another week and become an authority, a real authority, on basketball? Or a month and become one on football? After the game I stopped at my corner drugstore to whirl the book rack around. There between *Blood for Breakfast* and *She'll Do it Every Time*, I found the book I craved. *Winning on the Phone* by someone—you guessed it!—named Nixon. My heart jumped as I opened its red-white-and-blue cover. Here was the inspiration I needed, chapter by chapter: "How I Won with the Redskins," "Upmanship under the Basket," "Locker Room Sermons and Soliloquies," "Perspiration and Constipation," "Playing the Game for Fun and Profit." It was all there.

"Move over, Mr. President," I said loud and clear, "here I come."

4

The Greeny Summer and the Wicked Webworm

The lawns, Lord bless 'em! I lift my glass of local claret to the modest squares of green that have survived the summer. How well we know that most of this country is being masked under asphalt, cement, or Astroturf. Some day when we take the children to the Smithsonian for an outing we'll show them a patch of smooth green stuff, under glass in a far corner, and explain, "Kids, that's a lawn." Then we'll shuttle over to the Zoo to show them a cow, with udder, and so our contribution to American history will have been made for that day.

Currently the neighbors on my street vary richly in their philosophies of lawn. One is a tense perfectionist who jerks up every weed. Another pins his faith on science. He has a tough new grass which crowds out all weeds execpt the ubiquitous onion. But for eight months of the year his grass turns a dowdy brown (or as he says, more poetically, wheat-color); only in summer is it verdant. Another rejects his lawn; so, like a businessman growing bald, it alternates between lank strands and bare spots. Still another loves his lawn, leaning down to whisper compliments on its color when no one is looking.

I compromise. I'm content as long as some sort of green growth covers the ground. Mine is a moderate aim, so middle of the road as to seem blameless. Yet I'm a cause of discomfort to the neighbors. Not because of my lawn simply, but because I use the last hand mower in existence. When I cut the grass my mower makes small, old-fashioned sounds. The reel clicks quietly; nothing roars. The neighbors hope for the day when I'll trade up and come zooming out of my garage with a shiny power mower blasting like a 747 on takeoff.

I both like and admire my neighbors, though. The yearning for a handsome lawn that possesses most of them has a homely gallantry to it. For they are fighting the impossible fight, dreaming the impossible dream. Beneath their feet lurk as ominous a gang of enemies as we could imagine. Seen close they look nightmarish indeed, as they creep, crawl, buzz, or burrow. Though their kind may shift with the season, their number remains the same. It's always huge. What are the chief enemies now that summer is nearly done? I recite them from a gardening column in my nearby newspaper. Sod webworms. Chinch bugs. Billbugs.

Sod webworms—the very term chills me. The columnist is forthright in his warning. "Watch out for them," he writes. He describes vividly what they do. Sod webworms are the offspring of moths. Their eggs hatch into worms, which thereupon devour the grass blades late at night. I can hear them munching now. Growing bigger, they build webs around their squirming bodies. Growing bigger still, they build burrows beneath the grass, and then (I quote), "They chew off the blades of the grass, drag them into the burrows, and eat them." Shades of Grimms' fairy tales!

The chinch bug—as every schoolboy knows but I didn't— "injures the grass by puncturing the stems and sucking the plant juices." The result according to our columnist is that "the grass is killed, and only crabgrass and other weeds are left."

And the billbug? What the billbug does is so bizarre that it can't be described to a decent reader.

But the remedies, you ask, what about the remedies? I'm grieved to report that the gardening columnist is like the love-problem columnist. Both use prescriptive rhetoric with small practical value. Says the love-problem columnist, "*Make* your husband stop seeing that highschool harlot." Says the gardening columnist, "If the grass starts to turn brown, try immediately to find out the cause, and apply a suitable remedy before it spreads."

11

I've discovered that I read the gardening columnist not for his dire descriptions of the enemies which threaten my patch of green nor for his vague formulas for foiling them. I read him for his incidental wisdom. Such as: "All grasses look alike to the chinch bug when it gets really hungry." There's philosophy, I remark with admiration. As true for men or mice as for chinch bugs. When next I'm tempted to criticize the crude appetites of some of my colleagues (or my own for that matter), I'll keep in mind that when they're really hungry they'll gnaw on any kind of grass.

5

Steam Radio

Steam radio is what the snide telly-boys at the BBC term the old-style radio which some of us have loved. They sneer usually out of ignorance though sometimes not. Yet it had its own absurd fascination. So cluster around your father, you rotten kids, while he tells you what steam radio was really like.

It started for a lot of us with Rudy Vallee and the super-hetrodyne set. He came on the air each Tuesday evening. You twiddled half a dozen dials till you got him loud and clear. "Your time is my time," he sang nasally. If it was summer and you stepped off your front porch or marble stoop, you could hear him on sets up and down the street. Then there was "Amos and Andy." Right now this blackface pair would make any ghetto militant growl. But Amos and Andy schemed amiably and bickered mellifluously. Sample scheme: the Kingfish sells Andy a car with no motor.

The programs came in all shapes and several sizes. The other night I sat leafing through a pamphlet, "Radio Yesteryear," which listed many of them and added capsule descriptions. There were the soap operas, heard every afternoon. "Backstage Wife," for one, sponsored by Dr. Lyon's Tooth Powder. Its script invariably opened, "We present Backstage Wife, the story of Mary Noble, a little Iowa girl who married Larry Noble, handsome matinee idol, dream sweetheart of a million other women, and the struggle to keep his love." Or "The Carters of Elm Street," with one episode synopsized thus: "Mildred's mother has mysteriously left for South America. However, Mildred correctly suspects that something is wrong." Or "One Man's Family," sponsored by Tabson's Cold Remedy, now as dead as its program; the essence of one episode is that "Father Barbour is dejected because Teddy's engagement has been broken." Or "The Romance of Helen Trent," whose multiple complications are merely suggested by this skimpy synopsis: "Michael the Artist is in love with Helen. Julie is still in love with Michael. Ken, the Song Writer, is also involved with Julie." Get it?

There were the mystery and horror half-hours. The eeriest was probably "Lights Out." The title of one script tells the total story: "Cat Wife." You can supply the scenario. Yet "Lights Out" flourished because it played on the powers of the listener's imagination. You leaned toward your set, envisioning the horrors you could only hear. "Inner Sanctum" was another lurid lovely. A sample episode: "A woman has apparently returned from the dead, a box with $100,000 is missing, and the woman's idiot brother is found suffocated in the basement." Or "The Whistler." Or "The Weird Circle," one of whose episodes is "A horrifying story of a sadistic fat man who enjoys squeezing people to death."

Elsewhere on the dial you got music, often band music from the big bands. The roll call ranges from the eternal greats to those forever forgotten. Cab Calloway, Duke Ellington, Benny Goodman, Glen Gray, Jack Teagarden: the great are all here. But we also find Jack Berch and his Gulfspray Gang, Jan Savitt and his Top Hatters, and Phil Spitalny and his All Girl Orchestra (Featuring Evelyn and her Magic Violin). And in a special category, of those undeservedly forgotten, "The Chamber Music Society of Lower Basin Street."

Best of all, there was comedy. It ranged from the pleasant, unostentatious serial "Vic and Sade" to the big, expensive comedy hour such as "The Fred Allen Show," sponsored by Ipana and Sal Hepatica, with the Mighty Allen Art Players. In between: a delightful diversity. It included "The Abbott and Costello Show" ("Who's on First?"); "The Adventures of Topper" starring the droll Roland Young; "The Aldrich Family" ("Henry Al-l-l-drich!"): "The Ed Wynn Fire-Chief Program" with Graham MacNamee as announcer and straight man; "Lum 'n Abner"; "Here's Morgan," spontaneous and mordant wit from a comic now reduced to quiz shows; "The Great Gildersleeve" ("Throckmorton is running for Mayor and trying to get rid of his future mother-in-law at the same time"); "Fibber McGee and Molly" ("Molly starts kicking Fibber in the shins every time he exaggerates"); "Easy Aces"; "Duffy's Tavern"; and the bouncy "Eddie Cantor Show."

The list is so long and lovely that I ought at least to name a few more on it: "The Burns and Allen Show"; "The Edgar Bergen and Charlie McCarthy Show"; and of course "The Jack Benny Show" with Phil Harris, Rochester, Don Wilson, and Kenny Baker among those supporting the star—and the Jello singing commercials which made advertising almost palatable.

It was a very interesting era, kids, and I'm not just invoking the good old days. Even the moon looked bigger. Anyway, the end of the era came gradually, as television applied its crushing weight. No era ever ended on a certain afternoon; otherwise for this one it might have been the afternoon of November 11, 1960. The afternoon when listeners, a dwindling yet still faithful band, dialed in on "Oxydol's Own Ma Perkins." Speaking in her dry but kindly voice, "America's Mother of the Air" read them a message in this final program after twenty-seven years on the networks. The message was a mournful goodbye. The listeners dropped a tear or two, finished shoving the dishes in the dishwasher, and then switched on television.

6

Adam's Insight

I revive, for your inspection, my pet Polish count, Adam de Gurowski, accent naturally on the second syllable. He was, as we say of Tiny Alice, Something Else. He flourished in America during the 1850s, yet he has a message for us now.

He was born in Poland, had a highly unruly youth, was chased out by an apoplectic government, and fled to France. Thereafter he went to Russia, which he was soon invited to leave by its irate czar. Then he proceeded to Germany, Switzerland, and Italy, and finally to France again. In 1849 he came to the Land of the Free.

He headed for Harvard College, then in one of its stuffier phases, in the touching hope that he could teach there. Harvard reacted like a fat lady seeing a hair in her soup. Let me give you an idea why. Here is how Gurowski looked, as limned by the journalist Robert Carter in the spring of 1851.

Carter first saw him approaching on Harvard Square: "He was at that time forty-five years of age, of middle size, with a large head and a big belly, and was partly wrapped in a huge and queerly-cut cloak of German material and make. On his head he wore a high, bell-shaped, broad-brimmed hat, from which depended a long veil, which he used to protect his eyes from the sunshine. His waistcoat was of bright red flannel, and as it reached to his hips and covered nearly the whole of his capacious front, it formed a startlingly conspicuous portion of his attire." And underneath the veil he wore a pair of enormous blue goggles, the size of super Foster Grants but with an addition that could make a swinger stare with envy: glass panels at the sides as well as before his bulging eyes.

He swung, all right. Not the least of his innovations was answering the door naked, though it should be conceded that his appearance this way was less disconcerting than when he was dressed.

He did his best to support his habit (it was eating) but with small success till he persuaded Horace Greeley of the New York *Tribune*, who always had an itch for eccentrics, to hire him as an editorial writer. "It is a most delightful position," he wrote a friend triumphantly; "I can abuse everybody in the world." He did, on the paper and off. He said of the entire South that it had less intelligence and refinement than one New England village. He said of Abraham Lincoln that he was a beast, of William Seward that he was ludicrous. And so on.

The weird thing is that beneath the eccentricity and wild opinions lay a discriminating, broad-ranging intelligence. And piercing, penetrating eyes which, in this connection, needed no goggles at all. In 1857 he published what I'm convinced is the best book on America by a foreigner which appeared in the nineteenth century. Through his forced wanderings around the Continent he had made himself a student of comparative cultures, French versus Russian, for instance. After arriving here, he could use his observations as a superb context to set America in. He baptized his book *America and Europe*.

In it I believe he judges us fairly, without condescension. He says so many illuminating things that they could fill columns; let me say something only about Gurowski on women and then on the younger generation.

He finds the antebellum woman cultivated and reform-minded. He notes that her husband defers to her and even helps her by going to the grocery store: "the marketing . . . is generally within the range of the man's domestic duties." Yet she is colder emotionally than the European woman; Gurowski suggests, in a passage which has always intrigued me, that our climate is at least partly the cause.

He is at his best on the young. Taking a long, thoughtful look at them in Cambridge, New York, and elsewhere, he comes to some surprising conclusions. American parents, he writes, not only control their children less than do European ones but are actually meek toward them. "In America children generally lead and regulate their parents . . . in most of the relations and modes of life." Where is that birch-rod discipline we always heard about? Where is instant, old-fashioned obedience? The young make their own decisions in religion, politics, business, and—of course—love.

In our country youth dominates, no doubt about it. The result, says Gurowski temperately, is that "Society in America has thus a physiognomy of freshness together with a tint of harshness." He adds in an aside, which anyone can appreciate who gawks at female fashions or customs, that the young unmarried women set the whole tone for American social life.

Now what is there for us in Gurowski's acute observations? The salient thing I see is that, even then, ours was a youth-oriented culture, and that the older generation had abdicated to the younger. Of course this was less true in the 1850s than in the 1970s, and he was comparing America to Europe. But all that has happened is that, throughout Western civilization, we have all taken one step forward (or backward, if you wish). I won't forget the East German father I heard in Jena a couple of years ago complaining heavily that his son and daughter flout him. And this in East Germany.

So when we glower at our college students who trash and rebel and puff pot, we glower at nothing new. At times there is less rebellion, as in the Age of Eisenhower; at times there is more, as there is right now. But the headstrong child and the meek, permissive parent have long been settlers here. Next fall when hordes of new students debouch on our campuses, I predict they'll be more headstrong than ever. And with some justification, I hasten to add as both a permissive parent and a meek professor. But the point is that we have been talking about a trend deep in our culture—a trend that we can hardly control. I wish I could predict permanent peace on campus and a well-regulated generation of the young. I cannot. Maybe, though, when you see what your son or daughter, your beardy boy or string-haired girl, is doing in our confrontations you'll suspend judgment. For some of it is patently good. And maybe you'll be able to forgive the faculty for some of its idiotic ineffectiveness in times of crisis. Maybe. Anyhow I imagine old Adam would.

7

Riding the Clotheshorse

I stand before the full-length mirror in my bedroom and stare morosely at my reflection. It seems to me that I look like a semi-retired hustler from Fire Island. My loving, indeed doting, children have given me a gaudy variety of clothes for Christmas. Because they've given them I've got to wear them. "Don't you like them, Daddy?" they inquire anxiously. "Sure, I do," I reply with a radiant smile.

As a matter of fact I not only feel ridiculous, I feel physically uncomfortable. These clothes are an affront to the human form. In proof, let me peel myself like an onion for your edification. The outermost layer features a green knit shirt in a fancy lozenge pattern. The shirt sports a stand-up collar which at the top pushes into my chin and at the bottom reaches toward my navel. The collar points must be all of half a foot long. The body of the shirt clings cloyingly and I'm sure that it's soon going to be hard for me to breathe. PROF SUFFOCATES IN SHIRT—I can imagine the headline.

If you think the shirt is dire, let me tell you about the pants. (Pants—oh, simple word for a once simple garment!) Mine are a candy-stripe knit, with the stripes ranging from pale purple to deep fudge. Naturally the pants are hip-huggers. That means they come only half way up to my waist and have only a slippery hold on my hipbone. I always thought that clothing should have some relation to the human form and that a belt, if there is one, should run nicely around the waist. Not here. The brassy baldric my youngest gave me is buckled across what we might call, at best, my lower back. The pants constrict me when I stand up, as I do now before my mordant mirror. And when I bend over, they unman me. I feel like a Sheboygan bratwurst tied in two.

The pants are as tight around my thighs as they are around my hips. However, what their makers have saved in material in those parts, they lavished below the knee. For the pants bell out at the bottom till they nearly cover my boots. (Yes, boots; shoes are gone along with the Homburg hat.) I imagine that I'll be able to walk at least two steps before my trouser bottoms need to move. Pockets? Those indispensables for the male? These pants have only one hip pocket, on the left hip, into which I can barely shoe-horn my wallet. Into the two tiny side pockets must go: my jingling bunch of car and house keys, a collection of small change including a Canadian penny, my comb, a 3x5 card covered with notes to remind myself of things I have to do, a black engage-ment book, the stub of a pencil, a copy of Kipling's poem "If," three yellowed newspaper clippings tattered at the edges, a calling card from my friendly realtor, and a large pocket-handkerchief. Why not stuff this impedimenta into some other pockets, you ask? Because, friend, I don't have other pockets. My body-hugging shirt has none, and I don't have any jacket—the knits are supposed to keep me warm.

My sox are nonexistent but my boots would make John Wayne blush in embarrassment. They are chrome-yellow leather, gored at the sides, and with green tassels.

Let me peel the other layers of the onion quickly. Under my shirt I wear a green turtleneck whose collar folds three times. My underwear shorts resemble nothing as much as a male bikini. They're a brutal red, with "Straight Arrow" printed across the seat in blue letters. The innermost layer is my own old-fashioned stretch-skin; that at least has not been tattooed or transmogrified.

I take sparse comfort from the thought that at this moment hundreds of other husbands or fathers stand dourly before their mirror as I stand before mine. Who tricked us into wearing this

New Gothic, I wonder? Who sold our families and us the notion that at forty or sixty or eighty we should bedizen ourselves like preening bucks of twenty? By contrast the "sincere" styles of a decade and more ago seem almost sensible now. It's true that when you took a tall man, shoved him into a narrow black suit and snapped his collar tabs over a narrow striped tie, you had something like a walking pencil. He was really understated! But he wasn't a walking Christmas tree.

Even without Women's Liberation looking over his shoulder, no male dare pontificate today about the silliness of female dress. I know that most other societies like to costume themselves also, yet our clothing should have some sense to it. To advocate clothing reform is to make most readers yawn; it's hard to convert it into a crusade. Nevertheless, I urge Male America to demand at least a few improvements.

For instance. Shirts and trousers which are loose without being baggy and which follow the body structure but at a respectable distance. Shoes, not boots, like the old-fashioned "loafers." No neckties. No extra buttons (the shirt I wear has three on each cuff); zippers wherever possible. No so-called miracle fabrics; instead cotton from honest bolls and wool from contented lambs.

I can see me now. I stroll along the sidewalk in my reform attire. The eyes of onlookers widen. Here and there some fellow gawks while I walk in freedom. I enter a men's store, causing a commotion. An intelligent clerk rushes up to grasp my hand though the manager frowns in annoyance. At the male boutique next door, the goateed, fringed, and furbelowed salesmen look at my sensible suit with hostility. But I don't mind. Those of us who labor for man's betterment must bear an occasional jeer.

"Workmen of the world, arise," I announce, "you have nothing to lose but tight pants."

8

H. L. Mencken, Come Back

Dear Henry:

Forgive the familiarity. Though some of your ideas sound to me like an amalgam of Thomas Huxley and Horatio Alger, I'm convinced that you were a great man. We could certainly use you now. I know I've said that before but this time it's urgent. More of that, though, a little later, as they say coyly in the old pornos.

First I thought I'd report on some neighborhood news. The last time I drove over to Baltimore to your house, things were not all bleak. Hollins Street still had a kind of crummy charm. However, the house was crammed with people doing good. A few sticks of the old furniture stood around in the corners. Down in the cellar the vault remained intact, not surprisingly since its door still bore the red-lettered threat that any tampering would result in a faceful of chlorine gas at 250 pounds pressure. Though the back yard has been cleaned out, your brick wall with the Beethoven mask on it bulked just as solidly as you'd forecast it would.

In spite of the new order a touch of Mencken lingered in the air. Because your brother August had willed the house to the University of Maryland without any strings, it soon sheltered the School of Social Work's continuing-education project. When this was announced in the papers, it was feared that, ever after, you would roll around in your grave roaring and bellowing at the desecration. I doubt that you did, but if you did you can stop. I had a good talk with the sociologist in command of the house and I swear that his brisk New York accent was being overlaid with a layer of pure Baltimore.

I also had a talk with a bright young woman who was both living in the house and working there. Her bedroom was what used to be your famous front office. It seemed to me that she surveyed the goings-on around her with a beguiling blend of realism and idealism. And I glimpsed in her eyes that wonderful "What a circus!" look your friends detected in yours. Incidentally, she kept a volume of your *Selected Prejudices* by her bedside.

Anyhow, we need you. The nation is full of people who rail at it and there are those who genuinely hate it. A handful of the railers have a touch of black humor. But there's no one with a tenth of your wit, the wit that could compel us to assent, even to an outrageous proposition, with an unwilling grin. Your critical faculty was omnivorous. Toward the close of your career you stated proudly that you had never once praised a president. Wilson made you bristle. Harding—"the sainted Gamaliel"—sent you into fits of mirth. Both Roosevelts repelled you; as early as 1920 you tartly termed FDR an ass. Hoover was a cream puff.

However, you hoarded your choicest expletives not for a president but for the public who voted him in. Having given the matter solemn consideration, you concluded that the "American people, taking one with another, constitute the most timorous, sniveling, poltroonish, ignominious mob of serfs and goose-steppers ever gathered under one flag in Christendom."

Our newspapers need you most perhaps. The last systematic critic of the press was A. J. Liebling a generation ago. Now all we have are Mr. Nixon's thick denunciations. And they have totally lost the tang of novelty. There is an occasional single-shot critique in a magazine like the *New Yorker* or the *Washingtonian*. The Washington *Post* from time to time has named an ombudsman from its staff to police his own paper and to vet the press in general. So far, however, his tenure has tended to be short and his efforts feeble. The *Post* has also had a house radical, Nicholas Von Hoffman, who in his column is a slashing critic of anything far from home.

Not you. You were as willing to take on the press's glossiest mandarins, the Washington press corps, as you were the Reverend Billy Sunday. Today I must report to you that they still strut, even while sitting down. They still sun themselves complacently in the long afterglow of Watergate, forgetting that out of a corps of over a thousand, less than a dozen did the investigative reporting which broke the Watergate scandal. They still move in a cocktail-colored mist (they don't quite smoke pot yet), convinced that they control the country. They still, to quote you, "come in as newspaper men, trained to get the news and eager to get it; they end as tin-horn statesmen, full of dark secrets and unable to write the truth if they tried." Journalists in general? "Ignoramuses, and proud of it." And the editors and the publishers? They still richly deserve one another.

We need you now. However, I remember talking to Drew Pearson once and he said that if you were writing today, no newspaper would print you, including the New York *Times*. Perhaps so. Yet it seems a shame to leave the shortcomings of the press to the Nixons and the single-shot guerrillas in the class magazines. The most cogent criticism can be made from inside and it should be made by an insider as you made it, with love. For in spite of your rowdy polemics you loved the newspaper world all your life. You could look back joyously in *Newspaper Days* to your first job as a reporter: "I was at large in a wicked seaport of half a million people, with a front seat at every public show, as free of the night as of the day, and getting earfuls and eyefuls of instruction in a hundred giddy arcana, none of them taught in schools." And you relished your last job nearly as much.

We miss your zest; we miss your raucous commentary. Henry, wherever you are, come back. We've even shined up the old Remington and threaded a new ribbon into it.

9

Silphium for Your Sinus;
or, Up the Common Cold

The commercials come on and I stare malevolently at the Tube. The kindly, grizzled druggist peers at me from the picture, over his half-glasses, and urges me to rush off to buy Bayer's or Geritol or Carter's Little Pills. His tone of voice is totally reassuring, pure goose-grease, though his promises are conditional. "Just try it," he urges me, "and see if it doesn't work wonders." He holds out the prospect of a painless life, while I smile wryly.

However, I admit that he has a potent tradition behind him and an interesting future in front of him. My guess is that ten years from now he or his successors will be touting a favorite brand of pot in much the same way. Old Gold, Old Acapulco Gold, that is. Hymning it as do some of my students, he will expound on how it loosens tensions—"Smoke pot for a good party" —or induces calming meditation—"Helps open up the rich world within"—or stimulates the senses—"See and hear as you never did before."

Think I'm wrong? Look at the record. The history of patent medicine is a full one, adorned with anodynes, emollients, and elixirs. One of our favorites in the mid-nineteenth century was a widely guzzled "internal liniment" which must have been at least one-third alcohol. I'll bet it soothed. In the early twentieth century a farmers' favorite often cited by H. L. Mencken was Peruna.

It took years off the shoulders of the dirt farmer as well as his despondent wife. And some of us are old enough to remember what Lydia Pinkham did for the human race.

But this fanatic devotion to drugs is not restricted to America or its brief history of a few hundred years.

Take the case of silphium. When the Greeks sailed over to North Africa in 631 B.C. to colonize Cyrene, they encountered it there. It grew on the green hills and the colonist soon learned to export it and turn a tidy profit. No one knows exactly what the word *silphium* signifies, even our most knowledgeable writer on it, Chalmers Gemmill, whose 1966 article in the *Bulletin of the History of Medicine* is the place where I cribbed most of my esoteric information. However, a good many other things are known about it. For it soon became famous in the Attic world, as an Anacin of multifarious uses. It achieved an eminence that even the Madison Avenue flacks could never dream of for Anacin: its image was stamped on the coins of Cyrene, as the colony's coat of arms. What an advertising gimmick! Think of stamping Peruna on pennies or Dexedrine on dimes.

For those of you far cosier with botany than I am, I simply report that silphium was probably *Ferula tingitana*. Now you know.

What was it good for? The answer would kindle the eye of the most blasé of television pitchmen. It was a healing agent. It was a seasoning for food. A vegetable, it was a food itself. It benefited man or beast.

To be precise, it was recommended—in the works attributed to Hippocrates, a medico now in disrepute at the Johns Hopkins Medical School—for the proper purging of fever, for the elimination of abdominal pain, and for prolapse of the anus. Pliny announced that it healed skin diseases, removed warts, and dissolved painful corns. That wasn't all. He added that it had proved useful in cases of mange, coughing, quinsy, and sciatica. Columella asserted that it cured diseases of the eye. Apicius (yes, Apicius, doubtless the Julia Child of his day) maintained that it made a tasty sauce.

With such endorsements silphium remained popular during the whole classical era, on down to the Middle Ages. Greece

27

slipped and Rome fell; silphium marched triumphantly on. The Arab physician Al-Razi prescribed it for baldness, tetanus, toothache, piles, and expelling leeches from the throat. I stop only because of the risk of my overselling silphium. But I wouldn't be a proper American if I didn't add that it promoted sexual vigor.

Ah, silphium! When Antiphanes the charioteer left Cyrene, by request, he said sardonically, "I want to say goodbye to all horses, silphium, chariots, silphium stalks, steeple-chasers, silphium leaves, fevers, and silphium juice."

You can hear the commercial now. The buttery voice and confident tone of the TV announcer as he lingers over the silver syllables: "SILL-FEE-YUM." Whenever that commercial comes on, I'll turn off the Tube and hurtle to my friendly nabe drugstore to buy some, trampling the other customers as I run.

10

Selling Education in the Jazz Age

Many of us can remember, if dimly, the year the Great Depression began. (OK, not you.) And yet time has such a way, remarked by various prominent poets, of warping things that it can be almost startling to go back to the actual records. I'm reminded of this because I leafed last week through the end section of my *Who's Who* for 1928–29, which lies on our teakwood living-room table, as it does in every well-appointed home.

In aggregate, the ads make up an educational directory and they throw a beam of light on how some of our values have altered. Values are the trickiest thing to watch in any culture; they shift while we're thinking of something else. They are like some of the terms we use. I know that I still say icebox, though the iceman has gone the way of the passenger pigeon, and when we want our refrigerator repaired we humbly apply to the electrician. I can still talk about a *wrist* watch, though it's the only kind of watch my children recognize. I doubt that they've ever seen a pocket watch or even a lapel watch. I can still talk reminiscently about *the* war and mean World War II rather than the Vietnam disaster.

For anyone who balks at the belief that we've moved into a different world, let me cite a little evidence from the fat red volume for 1928–29. I begin with a bit of a shocker. It was a time when Wellesley and Smith, on facing pages, advertised for students! So did Mount Holyoke, which boasted that it had its own filtration and pasteurization plants. Among the men's colleges Dartmouth advertised; so did Duke, even though fat with "Buck" Duke's funds. It announced ponderously that it possessed "Noble Traditions." Notre Dame, for its part, announced that it had 154, count them, 154 professors.

Smaller fry felt it advisable to make other claims. Manch College in Virginia boasted that every bed was a Simmons and that its social life was highly attractive. In large type the University of Miami billed itself as "The Outdoor University," adding that it was always June in Miami. The slogan at Howard Payne College in Texas was "The School Where Everybody is Somebody," a theme not unknown to popular song. In Boston the Emerson College of Oratory promised the degree of Bachelor of Literary Interpretation to those pear-shaped students who mastered the course of study.

The preparatory schools advertised a buxom variety of advantages. My favorite is the Morgan School in Tennessee, which worked both sides of the street at the same time. It promised to encourage in its pupils both independence and obedience. Not far behind stood Sewanee Military Academy, which reported that it was a school of Christian influences, essentially military. St. John's in Wisconsin made the riskiest promise, for it declared itself "A School the Boy Will Like." The first advantage which St. Albans in Washington listed was that it lay a mere three miles from the White House. No doubt the idea of tea with Herbert Hoover had considerable lure for the parent who itched to give his boy every aid. The first asset listed by the Horace Mann School in New York was "close and comradely relations between boys and men." The Gulf Coast Military Academy sounded a variation on this theme by assuring the parent, "Send Us the Boy and We Will Send You the Man."

The emphasis in the advertising of the boys' schools is as much on character as instruction. The popular term for the kind of boy to be produced is "clean," though "square" is not yet unfashionable. No place went further in this direction than the Craddock School, which proclaimed that one of its objectives was to produce young men "Christ-like in Character." I wonder what school would be bold enough to advertise this today? Yet, though the

phrasing makes me squirm, I have a curious feeling that we ourselves should try to do something about character in our colleges,
even in our graduate schools. If you pinned me in a corner, I'd
probably concede that I thought a Ph.D. degree ought to result in
a better person as well as a better-trained one. To me, as an
amateur historian who sees more and more parallels between our
country and the later Roman Empire, the Craddock School has
something of a message.

Anyhow, at times the demonstration of how our cultural values
have converted is dramatic. In point, there is the military academy
in Los Angeles which assures the reader of *Who's Who* that its
student body is pure Caucasian.

And then there are the institutions which sent in their advertising copy with the best of faith, never remembering how slippery
words can be. For example, Southwestern in Tennessee, which
calls itself "A College for Those Who Discriminate." And Hebron
Academy in Maine, which will admit only students with the sort
of sight it calls "college vision."

But today we're no better. Though the rhetoric shifts, the sales-
man is still selling. The ads no longer run in *Who's Who* or in the
elite magazines. Instead everything is put together in the aptly
named college catalog. It lists all the course offerings but manages
to offer the expected lures as well. A decade ago a college president cast a penetrating eye on the catalogs of that time. He discovered, he reported to the waiting world, that most of the
colleges promised all the advantages of the country plus all the de-
lights of the city: though snugly rural they all happened to be
close to some notable metropolis. He discovered further that the
announced ideal of the men's colleges was to produce a well-
rounded man but that the women's colleges never once promised
to produce a well-rounded woman.

This year we're pushing—besides Black studies, childhood
studies, and transcendental meditation—relevance, venturesome
learning, and a grave respect for the psyche of the student. A
decade from now, I hazard, our catalogs will be merchandising
required courses, intellectual rigor, and the Puritan ethic. A decade more and we'll be half-promising to produce Christ-like
character again.

31

11

The Kitchen Mechanic

HAR HAR HAR! As Mencken used to say sardonically in his Free Lance column for the *Evening Sun*. Everyone recognizes the comic spectacle of the clumsy husband sweating and swearing when he's forced to work in the kitchen. We see it in the TV sitcoms all the time. Very funny? No, not very, if it happens to you.

My wife came home from the hospital the other day with instructions to stay in bed. So I got the chance to do the cooking—as well as the vacuuming and mopping and shopping. About time, you say, and you're right.

My first step was to slope over to the supermarket. As Ellen said reasonably enough, "If you don't buy food, you can't eat." So I went to our local friendly-food emporium and suffered a shock. The few items I bought, and most turned out to be the wrong ones, cost me nearly thirty bucks. Ellen said, "Bring home some lamb chops." I bought a couple at $4.19 a pound. First of all, I was irked at the .19 instead of an honest .20 and secondly I bought the wrong chops. They were supposed to be loin chops, Ellen explained when I got home, not shoulder chops. While I mantled visibly, she gave me a five-minute lecture on the anatomy of the lamb.

I'd already stopped at the drugstore and bought a cookbook

for idiots, a book of the "I hate to cook and I'm stupid anyhow" sort. Thus armed I strode into the kitchen. I was about to make a dish that a pink-cheeked child of ten could make, as the gabby instructions assured me. You just jumble together rice, beans, tomato paste (I know, who wants to paste a tomato?), two eggs, an anchovy, and a dire collection of spices (just a pinch of each), including oregano, the old hippie substitute for marijuana.

I spare you the gory details. Literally gory. A guy could get hurt in the kitchen, what with all that frying and burning and boiling and bubbling.

But what hurts most is not my burns but my male ego. The text of the book simply confounded me. It was evidently written by the wife of that enemy of the human race, the fellow who thinks up the put-together instructions for the toys you buy from Sears Roebuck. Without doubt English is only his second language if not his third—and he's glad. Also, I growled at such cheery little asides as: "Rice presents no real problems" or "Don't fret too much about noodles" or "This is so simple it's embarrassing." Or the grandiose lie about the results, "They all taste good."

I likewise object to the book's infantile strategies. It assumes that by giving a dish a cutesy title—Stayabed Stew, Idiot Puree, Sub Gum Yap—it makes it easier to cook. And it adopts a reprehensible mateyness of tone; for instance, potatoes are chummily called spuds. Then there's its cosy vagueness. "Fry the onion till it's tender." Isn't an onion tender to begin with? I've never in my life heard the expression "Tough Onions!" Or take the instructions about onions in another dish. "First drain your onions." Of what? I've drained a crankcase and a tankard of ale; but never an onion.

Another thing. Despite the fact that this book pretends to be so Now, it really betrays a cultural lag of thirty years. I'll bet it's true of the recipes and I know it's true of the point of view. To rip off an example: "A fact of life, like dilatory streetcars." When was the last time *you* waited for a streetcar?

I ended up by throwing the book into the Disposal, where it jammed. Returning to the drug store I bought a cookbook for bachelors this time. I've been leafing through it and popping an eyeball at its nude centerfold while Ellen smiles amiably. It has a few advantages over the idiot book but not many. And it has one added characteristic. Every dish seems to be concocted so that it's a prelude to sexual intercourse. First the dinner table, then the double bed. The dishes all claim to be spicy, intimate (you never cook for more than two), heady. Clearly they are to be cooked to muted Muzak and eaten to the sound of gypsy violins. But not cooked by me, nor eaten either.

But I'm boring you with my troubles, I'm sure. I might as well switch on TV and watch "As the World Burns."

12

Greatness at a Glance

The other night I switched on my FM set and there was Robert Frost reading "The Witch of Coös" in his ancient, tangy New England voice. Frost was alive again, the witch spoke wonderfully, and the poem was superb.

I thought of the time, some years ago, when I knew him best. He had agreed to come to England, under our government's auspices, to visit and to read his poems. I was the cultural attaché at the Embassy in London, on leave from my university; and part of my job was to help him while he was there. He arrived crusty and suspicious, playing Robert Frost to the hilt. He thought he should have been invited to stay at the ambassador's handsome residence in Regents Park; instead he had been consigned to a room in the Connaught Hotel. I went there half an hour after he'd registered, to see that things were going all right. He let me in agreeably enough, and just behind me stepped a pretty young woman from a London newspaper to interview him.

Almost as soon as she asked her first question, I noticed a problem for which my hasty diplomatic training had never prepared me. Robert Frost was unzipped. I decided that any attempt to signal him would make me look like a character in a Marx Brothers movie, so I sat back while the girl smiled nicely and made notes and Frost talked about his early days in England. When she

rose to leave he offered her, with a bit of a bow, a bouquet someone had sent to the room. I couldn't tell him about his zipper
after that.

His tour of England was a triumph. He received honorary
doctorates at both Oxford and Cambridge, the first American poet
in nearly ninety years to do this. He read, or rather, recited, his
poems generously; and the effect was like a bright October day.
And his personal style was delightfully free from cant. I recall, for
instance, how he dryly told a packed audience of Cambridge
students that the important thing was not what they learned but
the degree they won. Charmed by such Olympian candor they
drummed their heels and shouted "Hear, Hear!"

A couple of times I drove with him to his readings. From listening on those drives I discovered how wide and exact was his
command of British poetry of the past. He could recite not only
from major authors but from such minor ones as Sir Walter
Raleigh. And unlike some poets I've seen, he spoke their lines
with the same relish he showed for his own.

I was later assured that he was at his best during that English
visit. England had appreciated him before America; he never
forgot it. The English had long felt that he was a great man. Before them he grandly displayed the person of a Yankee seer, but
he peeped from behind the mask every now and then to show that
he appreciated his own performance.

To me he appeared most imposing at a dinner shortly before he
left, given at the English-Speaking Union for him and T. S. Eliot.
Here were the greatest American poet and the greatest English
one (true, Eliot was born in St. Louis but he had become English
to the core) at the same table. They sat talking with one another
in tones of the purest respect and affection.

Frost's stay was brief, covering merely three weeks. After he
left, and especially when recalling that dinner, I wondered about
something I still can't settle in my mind. Is it possible to detect
greatness in a person when you meet him or her? Eliot when you
spoke to him was simply an indifferent Buddha; Frost was a
sagacious, sometimes whimsical, sometimes fretful old man.
However, even his crotchets had a nicely individual turn to them
—as did his kindness: for example, on leaving he gave me a book

of his poems inscribed "Much beholden." Yet, taking all this and much more together, I couldn't be sure I'd met a great man. How could one be sure?

The answer lies mostly, I realize, in the public record. What poems has the poet published? Or—to take a Washington preoccupation—what laws has the senator sponsored? What deeds has the president done? The trouble is that at times our assessments shift startlingly. We once thought Longfellow's ballads grand; we once thought Melville's novels negligible. We thought Thoreau was a crank who stomped around measuring snow. We thought Harry Truman no statesman but a testy politician. Today I wonder about Lyndon Johnson. Will the people who made fun of Johnson's ears and accent seem, some day, as vulgar as those who a century and more ago called Lincoln the "Illinois Ape"? Or both?

Anyhow, on the record I consider Frost the greatest of our twentieth-century poets. And his finest poem? Not "The Witch of Coös," unforgettable though it is, but the sonnet "Never Again would Birds' Song be the Same," that Aladdin-like tribute to Eve. I wonder if you'd agree.

13

Tennis Tomorrow

It was at the Washington *Star-News* tennis championships. Cliff Richey, the defending champion, was playing Andres Gimeno in the second round. The tall, balding Gimeno took the first set from Richey and tied the second at 6–6. They started to play the "tie-breaker," that sudden-death innovation dear to the sports promoters. Gimeno won the first point. As Richey scrambled to the net for the second one, he caught his foot on the service-line tape, twisted his ankle, and bobbled the shot. He rubbed his ankle ruefully. Then as he walked back, he stooped, slid his hand under the tape, and ripped up the whole service-line. It was like a knife slash. We all gasped—we'd never seen this happen before—and then some of us booed.

As Richey limped off the court, Gimeno stared with a mixture of surprise and rage. After Richey plopped down at the sidelines to nurse the ankle, the officials swooped together like pigeons after popcorn. While they fluttered, the crowds in the stands discussed the situation. Several tanned tennis buffs near me declared that the feisty Richey should be forced to default. After all, it would take at least fifteen minutes for the tape to be pinned down again and for the court to be dragged smooth. By then Gimeno could easily have lost his edge. In the distance we could see him gesturing to the referee. It was a fair guess that he was saying exactly that.

We couldn't hear the officials' discussion of course but the drift was plain. When the court was in shape again, the loudspeaker announced the expected decision. The match would resume. Greed and showmanship had won over fairness. The paying spectators plainly wanted the match to finish, not least for the pleasure of booing Richey. They didn't have long to boo. Not at all put off by the delay, Gimeno won the tie-breaker and in ten minutes the match. Justice was served.

It will be a while before I forget Richey's tearing up that tape. But the angle that interests me most about the incident is not what it was but what it meant—or means. What does it tell us? Of all sports tennis is the last resort of (heaven forgive the term) the gentleman. The spectators act as a rule even better than the players. They applaud good sportsmanship and rarely boo bad. They sit quiet while the actual points are being played. In short, they behave themselves in, to me, an appealingly old-fashioned manner. During the first set a thatchy Texan near me was yahooing at each winning point that Richey, his fellow Texan, made. The crowd around him began to stare and he simmered down, though it took a little while. Decorum and discipline were restored.

Maybe we're better off for self-restraint. Admittedly, some of my college students don't feel that way, nor some of their elders for that matter. We can use ourselves as yardsticks. Have we become more disciplined or less in the last few years? I have a sneaky feeling that the answer is less. The young are showing us the way, in substance as well as style. They are as hairy as the mammoth but far more influential. I watched the president on television the other night and saw that the reports were accurate: his sideburns were longer by an inch and his hair was creeping quietly over his collar. When the shade of J. Edgar Hoover sports muttonchops the war of the generations will be over.

Still, I'll say a word for self-restraint, in fact more than a word. But maybe I'm wrong. Maybe our life today is so hemmed in, so cribbed and confined, that we need any outlet we can get. And maybe sports are our best outlet. Maybe we should embrace the player who gives us a chance either to cheer him wildly or to boo him roundly. Maybe the flashy promoters are right in scheming to give us "colorful" teams, teams we can hate or love. Who can hate—or love—the Washington Senators? But the Baltimore Orioles or the Colts? That's something else.

Perhaps Cliff Richey's analysis was the shrewdest. In talking with a newspaper reporter afterwards, he sized up the crowd's reaction. "They'll remember me not for my good tennis, but as the guy who ripped up the line. But they'll come back to see me because of this. Maybe tennis should be like baseball with the crowd. Maybe they should let them hoot it up."

Yet he also saw another side. When asked what concerned him about resuming the match, he replied that he was afraid some spectator would hit him over the head with a coke bottle.

14

Purer than Pure

I expect you've noticed how glossy my hair has been getting. And that I've grown heftier around the shoulders and leaner around the middle, and that I seem to be flexing my muscles all the time. And that my stride lengthens with a new purpose. And that my smile is more brilliant than ever.

Let me make the reason for all this perfectly clear. It isn't that I've taken to bolting down handfuls of Carter's Little Pills or Vitamin EEE capsules or to swallowing tablespoons of Snake Oil Extract. It isn't that I've enrolled in Vince's Health Spa ("Our sauna swings your September back to June") or have been yohoing on the parallel bars at the YMCA.

It's that I've finally started to eat organic foods. Organic foods, as even the check-out clerks now know, are grown without chemical fertilizers and processed without chemical additives. One of my daughters has long been an Organic Food Freak. With the tireless zest of a Muslim missionary she's been laboring to gather me into the fold. For quite a while she's been dropping newspaper articles on my desk about the dire effect of hexo-something or other. Whenever I've savored Maryland seafood she's talked to me about what mercury does to the human gizzard. While I've been peeling Florida oranges she's been pointing out the disconcerting fact that the orange coloring comes off on my hands. While

I've been salting my steak she's been reading the label of the salt-box to me in tones of doom.

I'm just about convinced. So, I recognize, are many thousands of others. More organic food stores open in my neighborhood all the time; the local health-food emporium which was teetering on the brink of bankruptcy is now abustle. Even the rather scruffy supermarket in the next block has seen the light. Deciding that if you can't beat 'em you gotta join 'em, it has made its organic food shelf swell into a whole organic food department.

Why not? The organic items seem to cost twice as much as the chemically assisted ones, though inflation has been narrowing the gap. The organic ones are plainly more expensive to grow but I'll bet that the markup is steep. A pound of organic honey—remember, you never use sugar for cooking; you use honey instead—costs me $3.79. A pound of peanut butter, my favorite spread, costs $3.77. A two-pound box of sea salt costs $2.65.

So I suffer, as do all of us poor, when I pay at the check-out counter. Yet the pain is eased by the thought of all the glossiness and vigor I'm gaining. Besides, I get a pastoral pleasure from reading the labels on the organic foods. "I, Otto Ogontz," a label on a lettuce box tells me, "to the best of my knowledge have raised this lettuce without an iota of chemical fertilizer." Otto, I believe you and munch your Emerald Iceberg with a hearty appetite. Other labels also smack of the idyllic life. For instance: "Balanced Sea Salt, Made from Sun Evaporated Sea Water." How reassuring the sun's evaporation is, how much better than a neon dryer! And I'm certain that the salt was packaged by contented workers wearing peasants' smocks.

The peanut butter, according to its label, comes from the Mennonite Country. Its ingredients are pure nuts and pristine salt, nothing else. The label intimates that this is "Nature's Way" and that the original peanut butter found on the African peanut-butter bush is merely more of the same. My honey is packaged by the Organic Food Corporation in Farmingdale, New York. Farmingdale isn't Mennonite Country but it sounds like the next best thing. "Farming" and "dale"—what an appealing combination! The label also bears the magic word "Tupelo," which I leave for you to riddle, as well as the portrait of a very busy bee.

No sex-starved hens have laid the organic eggs I addle. The cardboard carton standing on my sink says, "One Dozen Fertile Eggs from Free Running Hens Fed Natural Feed." These eggs hail from the henhouses of W. I. Wifmacher, also of Mennonite Country. I can visualize Farmer Wifmacher clearly, a stout man who watches his hens with a patriarchal smile while they run freely, with one of the roosters in hot pursuit. The eggs I buy now are laid by fulfilled hens, not nattering neurasthenics. The roosters, now likewise fed on organic feed, show a fresh gloss in their plumage; they haste to the henhouse with the highest purpose; and they impress everyone for miles with the brassy brilliance of their crowing.

Their strength is as the strength of ten because their feed is pure.

15

Saving Tara from the Kaldanes

Let me read a sentence to you from a much battered book. Gehk the Walking Head is speaking: "An hour since and you might have made your way to him; but now every avenue is strongly guarded since O-Tar learned that A-Kor has escaped to U-Thor." Pretty far-out stuff?

And another, this time from the author direct, describing how the stalwart Turan reacts to Princess Tara of Helium: "He felt his heart pounding in his breast and the hot blood surging through his veins as he looked at her beautiful face, with its downcast eyes and the half-parted lips that he would have given a kingdom to possess, and then he swept her to him and as he crushed her against his breast his lips smothered hers with kisses."

And one more, this time when the author is using all the resources of his rhetoric to tell us that a spaceship is in trouble because of high winds: "The groaning tackles bespoke the mad fury of the gale, while the worried faces of those members of the crew whose duties demanded their presence on the straining craft gave corroborative evidence of the gravity of the situation."

It would be unfair to keep you in suspense. Those gems come from *The Chessmen of Mars* by Edgar Rice Burroughs. My copy, rescued just ahead of the junkman, lies open before me. The covers have been nearly shaken off, the paper has yellowed, and the pages hold more than one reminder that as a boy I read and ate at the same time. And the harder I read the harder I ate.

Burroughs wrote the Mars series after the Tarzan series, and both series sold millions of copies. How could they? I ask myself now. The plots, even when their fantastic premises are granted, outrage probability. Princess Tara is blown thousands of miles across Mars by the gale and ends in a tower in Bantoom. Turan is blown thousands of miles across the same ruddy planet and ends, felicitously, in the very same tower. Moreover, he gets there just in time to save Tara from what I now recognize as rape. It ought to be added that I find, on rereading, that Tara stood in danger of rape throughout most of the story's 372 pages.

Burroughs cranks up his suspense in the most mechanical of manners. Here is a typical foreshadowing, the night before Tara is blown to Bantoom, "Nor little did she guess, nor her parents, that this might indeed be the last time that they would ever set eyes on her." Burroughs invites the reader again and again to feel gloomy forebodings though the reader knows in his heart, as Senator Goldwater used to say, that right will prevail.

Besides all this trumpery, Burroughs gives us a thesis; in fact he jams it right at us. It's that happiness comes only through a balance of body and mind. The first part of the story concerns Tara's travails in Bantoom (only the last part is about the fighting Chessmen of Manator and her struggle to preserve her honor from *them*). In Bantoom she falls, literally, into the clutches of the kaldanes—creatures who have been bred for nothing but brain and a pair of claws. Their vehicles are the rykors, who have been bred to nothing but body and are headless. Tara gasps with horror as she sees the kaldanes crawl onto the shoulders of the rykors and operate them. Recovering later, she reflects, "Between the purely physical rykor and the purely mental kaldane there was little choice; but in the happy medium of normal, and imperfect, man as she knew him lay the most desirable state of existence." In other words, let's not think too much. At the end she has convinced Gehk, the one friendly kaldane who has aided them. He admits that there are "finer and nobler things than perfect mentality uninfluenced by the unreasoning tuitions of the heart." Wild!

45

And yet . . . This tale and those like it found the millions of readers I mentioned earlier. I guess that Burroughs's stories appealed most to boys, and then to the boy in grown-ups. In those sexist days—*The Chessmen of Mars* was issued in 1922—there were many boys' books; and there continued to be, up to the 1960s. As a boy I myself took out from the public library every novel by Burroughs that I could snatch from the shelves, and that I hadn't bought out of my allowance. Then I'd run or roller-skate home and dive into a different cosmos.

Beyond Burroughs there were better books, though forgotten now I suppose. The sports stories of Ralph Heyliger for example, such as *Bartley, Freshman Pitcher*, which used suspense to inculcate character. I was a better boy, a better sportsman, after reading about Bartley. He played hard but never cheated—and he won. I took the lesson home. The historical novels of Joseph Altsheler on the American wars, from the French and Indian to the Civil War. And the historical novels of the Englishman G. A. Henty, crammed with adventure and seasoned with British battles, *With Moore at Corunna*, for instance. I would never have the faintest notion about Moore or Corunna except for Henty. I could lengthen the list. I relished them all. Perhaps they'd look as hokey to me today as Burroughs does. Even if they did, I suspect they'd be a vast improvement on the Boob Tube.

16

Meditation on Miss M

Don't bother. If you subscribe to the *Freep* or *Stone* you already
know what I'm going to tell you. At most I could merely tender
you a bit of validation.

But if you're like an editor who's a friend of mine, then I've got
some news for you. "Bet who?" he inquired when I mentioned
that I'd been to the Merriweather Post Pavilion in Columbia,
since we'd lunched together last, and had seen the best—repeat—
best—entertainer this country has today.

Bette Midler was superb, from the moment she skittered onto
the stage in her sleazy pink satin gown, which fought viciously
with her carrot-red hair. What vitality! She camped it up from the
opening number, not with slow, suggestive gestures but in a
frenzy. You couldn't call what she did singing. It was more than
singing; she was a skinny orchestra in herself. The result was a
string of songs, each different, each with its own belting rhythm,
and all marvelously varied in tone and texture.

What she did to "Chattanooga Choo-Choo" hasn't ever been
done before. That train bounced on its brassy track like crazy,
puffing out any number of small explosive clouds. Of course she
was helped by the Barry Manilow combo and aided and abetted
by the Harlettes, three ladies in the shade of the banana tree. They
bumped and ground like a coffee mill. At the end of "Choo-Choo"

47

Miss M simply flopped full length, all five feet one inch of her, on the stage while we stood up waving our arms or pounding our hands together. On the far edge of the spectrum, and a lovely example of her versatility, there was the Kurt Weill-Berthold Brecht ballad "Surabaya Johnny." It was haunting, beautiful, and moving even to the gaudy transvestites who had come to be seen rather than to see.

But I get ahead of myself. Let me say something about Super-Star's earlier days, or nights. Thumbing her way to New York, she snagged a job there singing in the second row of the chorus for *Fiddler on the Roof* and then played one of the saccharine sisters. It didn't take her long to exhaust that opportunity, so she snarled her pet expletive at the Fiddler, making him blanche beneath his makeup, and quit. Then for quite a while she suffered from the miss-meal blues. Finally, still toughing it out in New York, she found a job at the Continental, a men's Turkish bath. There she got to sing anything she damn pleased. She alternately smiled and snarled at her Byzantine audience, and they learned to love it. Manhattan's Gay community, entranced by her gamin quality— the old street-urchin bit—made her their prime favorite. Then she found other engagements, in between and elsewhere. She started to move around. She cut a couple of records, and then all of a sudden she had her own kind of national reputation. And, brothers and sisters, she has it now. When her concert, if I can call it that, at the Post Pavilion was announced it promptly became a sellout. The crowd not only jammed the Pavilion but covered the broad lawns behind it.

The sellout was justified. Her pace and timing have become perfect; her stage-managing is itself a work of art. Example: the way she exits at intermission, with her characteristic skitter syncopated to a triple beat. Example: the way she comes on again after intermission. The combo walks in first; the Harlettes sashay on second, now dressed as waitresses in what Miss M rightly calls "Howard Johnson drag." And then she jiggles on to join them all. Now she's wearing sleazy purple, ankle-length—and an apron. I can't tell you in these feeble words what a stroke of stage genius that dinky apron was. You had to see it. Same thing with the climax of that particular number. When the Harlettes simply can't sing any louder, they stop, fling open their waitress uniforms, and there is the American flag.

So next time scrape $6.50 together and stand in line. I vow it'll be worth it.

17

Under the Maryland Pigskin

In the bad old days when I arrived at the University of Maryland to teach American literature, we were universally famed for our football team. We had not only a parade of coaches but a coaching president. The best of them was Jim Tatum, who in his hot-eyed dedication to winning and the love-hate he aroused in his players reminded me of Vince Lombardi in his great Packer days. The president was "Curley" (he insisted on the "e") Byrd. There were vast areas of higher education, steppes and llanos of knowledge, hidden from Curley. Did he have any understanding of the liberal arts? Does a pig have wings? But football he knew. In College Park we couldn't help winning.

When Curley resigned, a new president, an ex-quarterback from Texas, was anointed. Winning football went on. A few of us on the faculty felt that enough was enough. I twice introduced in the university senate a resolution praying that we withdrew from intercollegiate football (I still own a copy) on the ground that it was of dubious educational value. You can guess what happened. The president acted as if I'd squirted him with soda water; some of my colleagues compared me, unfavorably, with Benedict Arnold; and I got a mere handful of votes each time. I remember debating the question with Jim Tatum's successor, a personable, smooth-talking Irishman named Tom Nugent. He out-blarneyed me by a statute mile.

Time passed, however, even as it does in "I Love Lucy." I gradually realized that I'd lost the battle but won the war. Football at Maryland began to slip and then to slide down a very steep slope. Several seasons ago the students at Harvard—they still had students then—voted ours the Worst Team of the Week. The football squad, not much later, itself dismissed its newest head coach.

This season, if you riffle through the sports pages, you know that Our Boys have seldom deviated into victory.

But this morning a remedy has reached my desk, in the form of a red-and-white flysheet. It has made my day and I share the contents with you, glad to give the newly forming Maryland Football Locker Room Club all the ink I can.

According to the flysheet the noble aim is to promote football at the university. The club already has a full set of officers, though none has a full first name. They are Joe, Dave, Pat, and Hank. The faculty recruiter is Dr. Jim. Subsumed beneath the noble aim, the twin objectives are to let the team hear we're still behind them and "to develop an *esprit de corps* among the fans within the state and the university community itself."

Already busy doing good, the club lists its initial accomplishments. It has bought a jacket and pair of pants for every player to wear on his trips. And it has paneled and carpeted the locker room. That, by the way, ought to shake the stalwarts of Curley's epoch. The locker room, in American tradition, is nothing but gray concrete and green steel, a suitable stage for the coach's growls, prayers, and curses when things go badly and hearty buttock-slapping and loud shouts when things go well. But who can picture any of this in a paneled, carpeted, chandeliered, and softly lighted parlor beside Byrd Stadium? And especially if the team has to be careful of its free coat and pants.

The plans for the future look enticing. They include hosting "a cocktail party and fingertip buffet" (with three kinds of fingertips) after the chief home games each season. They include a spring barbecue "where club members will have a chance to get to know team members on a more personal basis." They include publishing a Locker Room Club *Newsletter* "to provide members with insights of the football program." The annual tab: $25.

Put me down, Dr. Jim. Add my name to your list. Not because of your stated objective of *esprit de corps*, not because of the fingertips or the carpeting. But because what you're trying to do has a kind of primal innocence to it.

You're trying to recapture our coltish youth for us. Today's campus, with its trashing, its obscenities, its threats to much you believe in, can be ignored if you concentrate hard enough on an amiable era that never quite existed but came close to it. Then the autumn air was clear. Saturday mornings we could rake the leaves together in our back yard and burn them. We could stand lazily watching while the graceful, slightly acrid smoke drifted away without polluting a thing. And on Saturday afternoons we could go, armed with blankets and booze, to the football game. There, while we yelled and the cheerleaders jumped and the majorettes tossed their batons to the sky, our team would always and inevitably win.

18

Broad-Brimmed Words

I've spent this last weekend house-cleaning my language. I've been charging up the steps to the attic, throwing off clouds of linguistic dust as I rummaged and cleaned, and then emerging with a sneeze to carry down the things I had to get rid of.

But it wasn't easy. I loved some of that musty old language and I hated to throw it away. I thought I'd give the best of it to St. Andrews' Thrift Shop down the road. There simply wasn't any storage room left, and I'm always acquiring new things, from syntax to sofas to shirts, so a good deal of the old had to go. Yet I'm as sure as I sit here that some of it would turn out to be useful again.

I'll always lament my old broad ties, for instance. The fall after I gave them away, the pencil-thin ones I'd bought in their place slipped out of style. I haven't yet adjusted to the bellying breadth now in fashion—ties five inches across, that cover so much of a man's chest and stomach that he hardly has to wear a shirt. And they make up into clumsy knots thick enough to choke a Clydesdale. The old broad ties, on the other hand, were just right for me.

However, when I think about it I realize there's little point to using language every day which half your hearers can't comprehend. So I've junked even some of the irreplaceable items. "Hairpin curve," for one. How can you kids know, when you watch the road races on TV and Howard Cosell (my favorite Martian) says "hairpin curve," exactly what he means? I can see your grin as you demand, "Who ever pins hair?" Not you, old buddy, not you.

"No-man's-land" is another. I can find nothing better for describing a kind of anomalous gray area. But "no-man's-land" dates back to World War I. Or "Fascist," not just as a general term of abuse but with a specific meaning. It dates back to World War II. "Daddy, who was Hitler?" or "Daddy, what's a Fascist?" I can hear you asking in your treble.

Then there's "running board." Sure, it's kooky like the rest of them when you hear it first. Who ever saw a board running? Anyhow, they're all gone now, except on the Volkswagen. It has them but you wouldn't know what to name them. And "roadster" and even "convertible." And certainly "rumble seat." I can see the dudes (there's a revival for you) on the block staring at one another and muttering "rumble seat?"

The vocabulary of sex has at least two levels. At the lower one the old, old four-letter words have never lost their popularity; nothing to throw away here. In fact, thanks to the militants of campus and ghetto, their popularity has zoomed. I've heard them used in a faculty meeting; I've seen them used in the *Atlantic Monthly*. In both cases it was like a little old lady hiking up her skirts or a little old man strutting in snug blue jeans. At the higher level the more or less polite words shift with every zephyr. There was "necking." There was "petting," which included necking. There was "heavy petting," which went right up to the abyss. These were followed later by "making-out" and "surfing." Then came a few more terms, mostly I suspect local, and then we reached the 1970s and the Age of Anything Goes.

Incidentally, every now and then the use of a sex-slang word spreads to the innocents among us. I've listened to a very nice woman while she complained of "being shafted at the meat counter." What she meant, it turned out, was that she'd been forced to pay too much for very poor pork-chops. Then there's the verb "screw." Its meaning has become as diffuse as a cloud of smog. It now covers miles of new land and has hosts of new users.

There's one comfort. The Newer Generation won't have to do as much house-cleaning. My students definitely use fewer words today. They express more of what they mean through body language; through shrugs, looks, or gestures. The communion they crave appears more emotional than intellectual. They rarely prize a vocabulary which is both extensive and exact. I could go further. I think that they are half-suspicious of it: "He talks so well he can't be sincere." When Hubert Humphrey speaks on our campus, he turns off half the student audience, and not only because he was once associated with Vietnam. He's simply too fluent for them.

So long, Old Words. I hope that a kind antiquarian will pick you up for a few pennies at St. Andrews' Thrift Shop, take you home, and set you carefully on the whatnot shelf.

19

Private Lives,
Public Places

I turned to the society news and there she was. The golden girl, the white goddess in her black bikini. Though she is moving elegantly into middle age, Jackie looked as young and entrancing as ever. True, as Mrs. Aristotle Onassis she has not, for some years, been one of the Great Untouchables. Reporters can make snide remarks about her; gossip columnists can indulge in irreverent speculations; *paparazzi* can pop up from the bottom of the sea to snap her sunbathing nude. But she had once, as the wife and then the widow of a president of the United States, been beyond criticism.

Looking back I can tell when, at least for me, some of the sheen first rubbed off her golden image. It was when she tried to hire a biographer. I myself don't believe you should be able to hire a biographer any more than you should be able to hire a wife or husband.

The biographer in this case was that eminent alumnus of the Baltimore *Sunpapers* William Manchester. I got to know Manchester in 1964 when he was working on *Death of a President* in a tiny office at the National Archives in downtown Washington. I was gathering materials for a life of H. L. Mencken and he had written one which came out in 1950 called *Disturber of the Peace*. It had the benefit of help from Mencken himself, before his stroke, and was an exceptionally good job. It was not documented, however; you had to believe Manchester since he never cited a source. To him footnotes were fogyism. Yet time after time when I dug up his sources and could test the accuracy of his statements, he proved to be precisely correct. *Disturber* was a vigorous, brusque book and caught something of Mencken's own style. After this stimulating start I'd have expected Manchester to press ahead with more biography.

But no, or at least not yet. He was also a newspaperman then, with the newspaperman's classic urge to manufacture a novel. He proceeded in fact to manufacture several, of which *The Long Gainer* got the most attention. I have a covert love for very bad novels, those geraniums of literature, and *The Long Gainer* proved to be a splendid example. Its subjects, scantily disguised, were the University of Maryland and its lusty president Curley Byrd, the onetime football star who had made the long gains of the title. Among the many characters who moved stiffly across the stage, I choose one to represent the rest, "Daffy" Dix. She was the head cheerleader, who wore her blonde hair very long and always, always carried around her rhinestone-studded baton. You've already guessed what she was doing to the handsome quarterback and that as a result State lost the big game, 35 to 0.

Just prior to publishing *The Long Gainer* Manchester did return briefly to biography, this time with *A Rockefeller Family Portrait: From John D. to Nelson*. It was a slight, disappointing effort. But with *Portrait of a President*, issued in 1962, the year after *The Long Gainer*, he did better. It gave us an uncritical picture of John Fitzgerald Kennedy, to be sure, but its sprightliness and sympathy for its subject were both winning. On the basis of this book the Kennedy family commissioned him to prepare *Death of a President*.

If Manchester had any qualms about the original arrangement with Jackie and the family, he never shared them with me nor was there any reason why he should: I was a mere acquaintance. But the problem that exploded in the newspapers of the world when the book appeared was built in. It was the problem of truth versus taste.

To simplify the matter for brevity's sake, the biographer wants to tell, if not the whole truth then a representative part of it. He knows he could never put in type all the information about his subject, even if he could find it; the macrocosm lies beyond him. But he can make every effort to offer his readers the microcosm. If the subject of the biography suffered from sores or fits of rage or necrophilia, readers should learn about it, at the same time that they learn about his devotion to the people, his high moral code, and his unflagging efforts to bring about world peace. The family naturally wants the second and not the first.

As the British gadfly Malcolm Muggeridge has said about the kind of biographer a family craves, "He is content to survey the upper portions of the iceberg which is human personality, and to leave the four-fifths under the water largely unexplored." That was the basic tradition of biography in English throughout the Victorian era. It once caused Thomas Carlyle to exclaim, "How delicate, how decent, is English biography, bless its mealy mouth!" Traces of this tradition still linger.

When a major political and personal disaster is to be explored in depth, I believe that nothing that has been discovered should be left unsaid. Biography expands into history. In the Kennedy-Manchester controversy which raged about *Death of a President*, I think that Manchester was entirely right. The reasons for the hot contesting of episodes, incidents, and details have already been forgotten; the book itself is standing the test of time.

And yet my heart went out to Manchester during the controversy, for there are occasions when being right is not enough. Sir Walter Raleigh observed, some 300 years ago—and I throw in this third quotation free—"Whosoever in writing a modern history shall follow Truth too near the heels, it may happily strike out his teeth." I trust not; there is no gloomier spectacle than a toothless biographer.

20

So Long, Lions;
Goodbye, Moose

OK, call me Jeremiah. But listen a minute; the Tube will wait while I lament the disappearance of Lodge Night not simply for itself but as a symbol. It has sunk to the muddy bottom of American civilization without a trace of a trace.

So gather round again, you rotten kids, while I tell you what you missed. A hundred years ago every small town had its couple of lodges; every big town boasted a considerable cluster of them. They had cryptic initials, with never an acronym. The IOOF, for instance, or the MWOA: the Independent Order of Odd Fellows or the Modern Woodmen of America. A century ago they donned gorgeous uniforms for meetings or parades. Shiny tin helmets, pants with red braid down the seams, epaulets with enough gilt to make a martial dazzle. They shone like Carpathian cuirassiers come to Peoria, as they marched in all the holiday processions, often with their own brass band blaring away. Every Wednesday night they held their meetings rich with ceremony and ritual, and these ended customarily with just enough alcohol so that the members could stroll home refreshed but not intoxicated.

A century ago there were prosperous factories in New England (yes, New England actually had prosperous factories) which did nothing but manufacture regalia. Today little is left. The Shriners perhaps, who wear their fezzes and blue bloomers with a forlorn jauntiness. They still wheel or strut at our rare parades but now they look camp. The Elks, the Eagles, the Moose? Their tribes decrease. The older members get gout and the younger members fail to show up after the second session. Like the American Legion, they have a dying air.

And nothing—this is my point—nothing is taking their place. What we call in sociologic jargon "voluntary institutions" are eroding week by week, month by month. Not only fraternal orders but churches, social clubs, mutual-aid or mutual-interest societies. In this country the church has been a voluntary institution for the last 200 years. I go to St. Andrews in College Park. It's now half filled on Sundays and the pews once crowded with university students (especially at exam time) stand vacant. I speculated for a time that St. Andrews was a special case, till I visited other churches and synagogues and temples. They are all hurting. Even the Rock of Rome has been splintered at one edge; I never thought it would happen but it has, partly because of abortion. And the Protestant denominations are either struggling frantically for relevance or retreating into a new fundamentalism.

The forefront of the struggle lies, I feel, on university campuses, and the struggle is going against us. On my own campus a marginal minister holds a psychedelic service, my students say, which he dubs "Celebration." Students come by the hundreds—once or twice.

The fraternities and sororities in my campus are shrinking too. In my student days I belonged to a typical one, structured by secret ceremonies and WASP prejudices. We addressed the head of our chapter as Worthy Master and we scratched three times on the sacred door for admission to the fane. It was weird. But the ritual included some lofty statements on behalf of brotherhood, purity, and service. And these weren't all cant.

Service . . . That reminds me. About all that we have left is the so-called service clubs which meet for luncheon once a week. The Rotary, the Kiwanis, the Lions, I know about. Also I remember the Optimists. Are there any Optimists left, I wonder? Do they band together, trying with false cheerfulness and resounding slaps on the back to make up for their dwindling numbers? And the others. Do they still have dish-sized nameplates (first name only of course), communal singing (starting with "God Bless America"), and a ten-minute inspirational speaker from the outer dark?

All these clubs have, or had, projects, some of them worthy and the rest probably harmless. They Do Good. What worries me, as I said, is that nothing takes their place. With a solitary—and to me dire—exception: the government. More and more of the services these institutions performed are either being eliminated or being taken over by the government. The urban Community Funds are sweating to fill their quotas and some are desperately cutting the quotas back. In competing for the few dollars which do dribble in, the whites claw at the Blacks and the Blacks claw at the whites. Nobody wins.

You know what we're heading for? Government churches, lodges, welfare societies. Government giving and inevitably government taking. I concede that I view the prospect with alarm. I'm convinced that the quality of American life is growing worse at an appalling rate. I recognize that it sounds cheap to say so, but I really do believe that 1984 is coming faster than we thought.

21

A Walk in the
Wonderful Sun

I rise to mark, this month, a neglected anniversary. That it has been forgotten is understandable; to many who took part in the Freedom March on Washington in August 1963, it is already as far away as the first automobile. As I myself think back it seems almost pastoral. Not so, then. Our instructions beforehand were explicit: If anyone yells at you or throws things, don't even turn your eyes; march straight ahead and look between the shoulder blades of the person in front of you.

But we never had to. I was in the line that marched along Constitution Avenue. We went twelve abreast, singing and carrying signs. At first I felt too dignified to carry one, but as we moved along in this tremendous parade, the spirit caught me. I was marching next to one of my children and I announced, "That sign's too heavy for you." With the selfishness of euphoria, I appropriated hers and shouldered it the rest of the way. As we marched, watchers on the sidewalk felt the pull and stepped off the curb to join in. Two hundred thousand of us assembled at the end of the Mall and heard speeches and cheered and ate. The weather was sunny but fresh, the best a Washington August could offer.

That afternoon we saw a sort of Utopia. I shall always remember it. Everybody, except for a few beatniks, was dressed up.

Everybody was kind to everybody else. We were all so good, and the day was beautiful!

It seems ages ago, this pastoral period of the civil-rights movement. Now we have Black Power, with its grim assumption that any march can turn into a riot. Black Power, ready to match the excesses of every Southern bigot.

And yet I believe that this Black Power stage of the movement is inevitable and, indeed, that good will flow from it. It is probably the coming of age, not only politically but psychologically, of the Negro. Perhaps this sounds condescending; I don't mean it that way. For the Negro, who has been imitating the white man, is starting to insist on his Negritude. And the Negritude is symbolized by blackness and sanctioned by the slogan Black Power.

In politics it means the drive for a bloc vote. To paraphrase a Cleveland leader, it means shaking the Negro into political action and making him vote collectively. In psychology it means—to begin with, if only to begin with—getting the Negro to purge himself of his own worst prejudice, the prejudice against a black skin. Any observer of Negro society knows the favored position that the light-skinned Negro has always had. In many a Negro neighborhood he has been allowed to feel that he deserves the best. The snobbery on the campus of a Negro college can make a white one look almost egalitarian.

The vogue of the bright-skinned Negro has been—and still is—abetted by the mass media. The day when a dark skin and Negroid features look good to the whole Negro community has not yet come. Stokely Carmichael still sounds a bit shrill as he exhorts the sharecropper, "When you see your daughter playing in the fields, with her nappy hair, and her wide nose, and her thick lips, tell her she is beautiful." But the day is coming.

Meanwhile, Black Power has work to do. Organizing the Negro into a political unit will not be easy and yet it can be done. That is the main job, important, obvious, and external. But the spread of Negritude is necessary too and its first target should be skin snobbery. The evidence is all around. On the inside cover of *Jet* a splashy advertisement urges "Have an ultra light, ultra bright skin"—use our magic ingredient. And *Ebony* advertises "A New Kind of Hair Straightener for Today's Kind of Man." If you don't like the term "straightener," other advertisements can offer you hair "relaxers." And these Negro magazines are models of restraint in comparison to the hard-sell advertisements clamoring that they can make you whiter than white.

Nevertheless, we are moving into a period when those things will be less important. We are moving into an age of Negritude and confrontation. But I look to the time when this too will pass and we will have the Utopia of that August afternoon when everybody was good to everybody else.

[Few things have changed as much as the civil-rights movement. Writing in August 1966, I looked back three years to the March on Washington and then forward to the final years of the 1960s. I thought I saw a Hegelian pattern. Its thesis was Black equality through integration. Its antithesis was Black superiority through separatism. Its synthesis would be a biracial Utopia where everyone would be taken on his or her own terms. I still believe that I caught a glimpse of that Utopia on August 28, 1963. I've kept this column as I first wrote it, in the hope, as I said in my preface, that it has a mild historical interest—and that it preserves some of the thinking and feeling of one liberal in the mid-1960s.]

22

Post's Bad Boy

Our prime exponent nowadays of the Bad Boy school of journalism is Nicholas Von Hoffman of the Washington *Post*. Having pored over his columns, I'd naturally acquired a mental picture of Nick (he'd want you to call him Nick). I visualized a wiry young fellow, black hair tangled and beard bushed, who typed with a bitter grin as he sat in his pair of New-Left overalls.

Last week I met him for the first time. I'm still picking up bits of blasted illusion, for Mr. Von Hoffman is middle-aged, gray, and heavyset. He wears a business suit. It came to me, when I mulled over this contrast afterward, that there was also a difference in his writing between appearance and reality. He writes like a Bad Boy, with violent wrenchings of language, but what he says isn't very bad. He's at his best in beating up paper tigers. He's actually—I pause for effect—a crypto-conventional. From Kansas.

The other morning I published this wicked accusation in a letter to the *Post*. By now, stung by my charge, several of his friends, his three admirers at the *Post*, and his cousin Eunice from Olathe, Kansas, have written me in outrage. Nick is nothing of the kind, they exclaim with more indignation that evidence. They allege that I harmed his feelings and made him talk of quitting his column.

Since I'm challenged, I want to put my evidence in black and white for all to see. Frankly, it's damning. I can prove that at this very moment he's a clandestine member of Kiwanis, a practicing Elk, and a paid-up subscriber to the *Reader's Digest*. But his past history, as we call it in Kiwanis, looks still worse.

In gathering that history I gratefully acknowledge the help of Col. Irwin I. Irwin, whose office over in Arlington has no plate on the door. Here is some of the early data, starting with Mr. Hoffman's boyhood, before he acquired the "Von," in Kansas.

1929: at age ten won American Legion "Boy Orator" contest for Olathe. Used the term *Old Glory* in every second sentence. Advised audience that what made America great was hard work, high morals.

1938: graduated from Benjamin Birddog High at Olathe. Cheerleader. Editor of the *Bird-Dog*. Captain of the debating team, which reached the state finals with "Resolved: that socialized medicine is sinister." Photo in yearbook shows him with eyes glassy, smile a dentist's delight, and black hair in pompadour. Caption under photo: "Old Nick—he sure can smooch."

1942: graduated in Christian journalism from Bob Jones College . . .

His dossier since college has been so full that I can only pull out pieces here and there. I give them in random order, for they all suggest that he's straight.

Judge in Miss Teen-Age America contest; picks the blondest blonde . . . Flies American flag from front porch . . . Front lawn has purple glass globe on pedestal, pink flamingo, and Disney's Seven Dwarfs . . . Owns complete set of *Encyclopedia Americana*, with loose-leaf inserts . . . Designated Dad of the Year by the Married Mothers of Cleveland Park . . . Recipient Junior Chamber of Commerce silvered medal: To Man Who has Done Most to Clean up Prince Georges County . . . Likes hunting (quail) . . . Favorite breakfast: Crunchies . . . Favorite dinner: steak, French fries, green peas . . . Originator of bumper-sticker slogan "America: Love It or Leave It" . . . Favorite author: Nicholas Von Hoffman . . . Next favorite author: Ayn Rand . . . Successively program chairman and president Cleveland Park PTSA; program theme: Positive Living in Progressive Washington . . . Foreign honor, from Croatian Government in Exile: Order of Chastity, Fourth Class . . . Picked by pressroom gang at *Post* for its Permanent Paper Hat award . . .

Had enough? Then join me in saluting Nicholas Von Hoffman as One of Us.

23

The Bookmakers' Helper

Though it hurts me I'd better be honest. This is not about Saratoga or Laurel or Pimlico. I can't give you a tip on the Whitney or the International. I can't give you the code the tic-tac men use at Ascot. My bookmakers aren't as rakish as others by a long shot (excuse the expression); but they are, I think, more valuable.

You look at the *Smart Set*, one of the great magazines when George Jean Nathan and H. L. Mencken coedited it, and the pages break as you turn them. The paper is yellowed, stiff; it smells of age. But you can go to any rare-book library, open a folio 300 years old, and look at pages smooth as cream. The color is light, the leaves flexible.

What happened? And does it matter? What happened is that American book and magazine publishers—my bookmakers—discovered in the 1860s that a cheap, seemingly satisfactory paper could be made out of wood pulp instead of rags. They made it, smiling fatly. The chief trouble was that it turned out to have a high acid content. The mysteries of paper chemistry lie beyond me; all I know is that such paper is what the *Smart Set* was printed on, and such paper is the reason the *Smart Set* is brittling and crumbling.

Is what happened of any importance? If you believe in history and the continuity of a culture, yes. For the books and magazines with nearly a century of recorded civilization in them, and all printed on this pinchfist paper, are shaking apart. So are the newspapers. If you appreciate the past for its own sake—and it has a certain quaint charm—or if you hope that we can learn something from the past and so improve the future—and that idea has a certain charm too—then you realize that we must save the records of the past.

Perhaps surprisingly, something is being done. The leader in the plans for the salvation of the past and the preservation of the present is an organization called the Council on Library Resources.

Smother that yawn. I know that certain words or phases turn us off. For me "culture" is one, "scholarship" another, "urban redevelopment" (forgive me) a third. It doesn't matter whether they mean good things or not; the labels are boring. "Council on Library Resources" is such a label. On the other hand, anything with the word "sex" in it will make many of us sit up. In fact I can give you an unbeatable title for an article, "Sex and Violence in California."

The Council on Library Resources is actually a jewel, one of my choicest organizations. It is financed by Ford Foundation money (after all, the Ford Foundation can't do everything wrong) and it has given much of its attention to the paper problem in recent years. There have been articles on this problem but none, to my way of thinking, has given enough credit where credit is due. The council early discovered a genius in, of all places, Richmond, Virginia. He was named W. J. Barrow; he was a self-taught paper chemist; and the council commissioned him to find out if the paper situation was as bad as it looked. If you relish meaningless statistics I now have one for you. As a result of Barrow's early studies it was found that the printed materials quietly decaying in American libraries amounted to 3 billion pages.

There are two main things the Barrow Laboratories have been trying to do. One is pretty well accomplished, and has been for some time. The other needs more work. The first is to develop a paper which today's bookmakers can buy at a moderate price and to make it as permanent as the beautiful Renaissance papers we admire. That paper is now available. It's true that it won't be used for *The Valley of the Dolls* and its busty successors, but many publishers are venturing to use it for books they trust will last. The second is harder. It's to take the *Smart Set* and a myriad of other crumbling items and put a preservative on them. It's always more difficult to correct something than to make it right the first time (I offer you this bit of homebrewed philosophy free). The problem of preservation involves all kinds of complicated steps. Many of them demand hand labor, currently the most unfashionable kind of labor we have.

Notwithstanding, the effort is under way. The years from the Civil War to the Vietnam disaster may not drop out of our history anyhow. And today's history—gaudy and horrendous as it is—will be preserved for the future to marvel at. I consider that the council can take a sweeping bow. Come to think of it, it's helping to fight the pollution of our intellectual environment. What could be more relevant!

24

Harried Chests

The male centerfold is one of the current artifacts of our culture. Pioneered by *Playgirl* and a couple of the still blowsier magazines for women, it leaves no stone unturned of the male anatomy. The highlights of the frontal view, from the female standpoint, include I'm told the chest hair. But once again, science has been there first. This time, though, in a guise which won't cause those of us in the humanities any pangs of envy, the guise of a perfectly sober scientific article. Now let some scientist accuse our studies of being tasteless or trifling!

Yet the article is so sterling a piece that I can't forbear sharing it with you. (Those of tender tastes can turn the page.) I even have an offprint of the article, secured at no small expense.

The offprint, suitably attired in a flesh-pink cover, is from the *American Journal of Physical Anthropology*, where the piece first appeared. It's the work of a Washington doctor I'll call Cosmo Blinn because, as the *New Yorker* likes to say, that's not his name. The article is entitled "The Distribution of Chest Hair in Caucasoid Males." It dives right into the subject. Not as in the humanities, where we usually indulge in a bit of foreplay before getting down to business. Cosmo Blinn is all business from the outset. I quote his initial sentence: "Danforth and Trotter ('22) considered two grades of pilosity in which the chest hair was the crite-

71

rion: grade 1, hair in the center of the chest or about the nipples; grade 2, considerable area of hair on the chest and breasts." How about that! I can't keep from going on to quote the rest of the paragraph: "Miller ('31) accounted for human hair patterning in general as a tendency imposed by primate heritage. Dupertuis, Atkinson and Elftman ('45) classified chest hair simply as sparse and conspicuous."

If you're a scientist you can't get away with dividing all herbiage into simply sparse and conspicuous, so our doctor moved in hard. I give his own explanation of his method. "The subjects observed," he says, "were stripped men in the shower rooms of public swimming pools in and near the District of Columbia. Selection was limited to adult, mesomorphic Caucasoids; but these were taken at random."

In the course of his researches Cosmo Blinn reports that he peered at no less than 310 chests. With that imposing number he was able to establish ten classifications. And not simplistic ones like Dupertuis, Atkinson and Elftman's sparse or conspicuous. His went up a ladder of rhetoric which Shakespeare could have envied. The progression was almost superb. Or rather the two progressions. Here is the first: Pectoral, Pecto-Sternal, Pecto-Infraclavicular, and Pecto-Sterno-Infraclavicular. The second is more splendid still: Circumareolar, Circumareolo-Sternal, Circumareolo-Infraclavicular, and Circumareolo-Sterno-Infraclavicular. Try saying some of those at the close of a long day. They're as tricky as my pet Scottish tongue-twister, "The Leith police dismisseth us."

In case you're counting categories on me, the two I've omitted are the simple Sternal and Infraclavicular. Anyway, all ten are drawn in the offprint, in what looks to me like the primitive ancestor of the *Playgirl* centerfold. The unknown artist (Blinn himself?) has lavished care on every chest. The dots of hair range from a little cluster on the center of the chest (Sternal) to a lush furring over much of the torso (Pecto-Sterno-Infraclavicular).

But I know that you're itching to hear what the findings were. Dr. Blinn discovered that the least frequent types were Infraclavicular, Pecto-Infraclavicular, and Circumareolo-Sterno-Infraclavicular, each with only 1 percent. The most popular by a broad margin was Pecto-Sterno-Infraclavicular with a smashing 51 percent.

It's been more than a decade since Dr. Blinn reported his researches to the *American Journal of Physical Anthropology*. I wonder if later scientists have disputed his results. Have there been bitter battles over the nomenclature or the source of the samples? Or has the article been accepted as definitive, and is the doctor proudly presented as "our chest-hair man"? Has he done a book on it, I wonder. Or has the cream of his research been skimmed for the luridest passages of *The Senuous Man* or for the steamy background of *The Sensuous Woman*? Does the sensuous woman stare avidly at the sensuous man, murmuring half to herself, "Circumareolo-Sterno-Infraclavicular"?

Me? I'm a wishy-washy, middle-of-the-road professor. I'm Pecto-Sternal.

25

The Pyramid and
the Beads

Look around you. You still see the Wild Ones getting all the ink. The newspapers remain as intoxicated with the counter-culture as does television. They prefer, any time, the shaggy youngster who cavorts with his pike-pole to the thirtyish supermarket manager on his way to work lugging a plastic briefcase. They happily report or record the guerrilla theater being played on the city streets. But their reports, I suggest, are getting moldy and out of date. Also there's a lot in the total cultural scene that such reports miss.

The most dramatic thing they miss is what you might call the counter counter-culture. I've just come from one of its deepest caverns. To be exact, from the training room, in Byrd Stadium, for the University of Maryland's athletes. I had twisted my knee playing tennis. Aware that no doctor would bother with me, I hobbled over to the training room and introduced myself. Al the trainer deposited me in a whirlpool tub and set the timer for twenty minutes. As the minutes ticked by, I surveyed my surroundings and soon felt like an archaeologist who has just broken into a royal Minoan tomb.

The discoveries were on the walls. The room itself is not exceptional. It's painted in glaring red and white and smells of antiseptic. Under the windows along the east wall, a row of taping tables stretches out. Against the opposite wall stand cabinets for gauze, tape, and elastoplast.

On the wall above the cabinets nine posters have been pasted, simple sheets of red with plain white lettering on them. Each bears a slogan designed to inspire the damaged athlete as he sits here being repaired. The authors of these inspirational sayings are not given, with the one exception you might have guessed, the late Vince Lombardi. In the Lombardi quotes you get the pure essence; in the anonymous ones it's watered down. Here are two of the slogans. Which, I ask you, is real Lombardi and which is imitation? One advises, "Fatigue Makes Cowards of Us All." The other says, "If You Can't Play Hurt, You Can't Play." No problem, right?

But the slogans are merely bits and pieces. The whole religion is synthesized in a massive poster on the north wall. The poster pictures a stepped pyramid, to the joy of the archaeologist. Each step has the name of a quality lettered above it and above the apex itself there glows the word SUCCESS. Though the pyramid is credited to John Wooden, UCLA's famed basketball coach, I'm convinced he speaks for the whole counter counter-culture. The qualities emblazoned on the left side of the pyramid leading upward to Success are, step by step: Ambition, Adaptability, Resourcefulness, and Faith ("through prayer"). Faith shares the top step of the Pyramid with Patience, both lying just below Success. Going down the right side of the pyramid, following Patience, we find Reliability, Integrity, Honesty, and Sincerity.

If this isn't the Protestant Ethic, beloved of all Puritans past or present, Catholic or Protestant, I don't know what it is. It preaches a way of life which our ancestors honored and which our descendants will probably spurn. It preaches strenuous effort and endurance, aggressiveness and enterprise. It preaches a life of both faith and works. It speaks with the oddly but harmoniously mingled tones of Cotton Mather, Benjamin Franklin, and Horatio Alger.

Yet, on second thought, our descendants may not spurn this ethic anyhow. For, as I suggested earlier, the counter-culture is itself altering and at this very minute. I made my way through the little psychedelic stores next to the University campus, searching in each one for significant slogans and posters. Talking with the exotic salesmen and proprietors, I got some surprises. They agreed that obscene slogans aren't selling as well as they once did. The market for four-letter shock words is shrinking. So is the market for satire. This, incidentally, I regret, for the black humor of the psychedelic posters has often appealed to me. Of the few older slogans still kept in stock, none was brutal: "Peanut Butter Power," "Stamp Out Pay Toilets," and "Let's Lock Loins."

What was selling fastest was Utopianism and mysticism. The bitterest militants now regard the sloganeering posters, old or new, as mere Mickey Mouse. Obviously. The shaggy bombers of the Far Left/Right couldn't care less for "Make Love Not War." After all they themselves have chosen war. For the average young cash customer the case is different. The star item in one store, the proprietor told me, is "I Believe in the Sun Even When It Does Not Shine." The next: "Today is the First Day of the Rest of Your Life." In another cubbyhole of a shop the most salable item was the Thoreauvian "To Enjoy Solitude is to Enjoy Freedom."

One odd, emblematic poster I found hard to forget. It pictures a gentle, unclad girl looking out over the Pacific sands, looking I think for Avalon. The caption is the single symbolic word "California."

26

Chow Time; or, A Modest Proposal

The commercial comes on. Bruno Boy bounds into the picture waving his shaggy tail (when you've got it, flaunt it) and slobbers on his master. Master looks up at us and announces, "Doesn't your dog deserve the best," while he holds out the can of Frisko Dog-Bits to us with urgent admiration.

You feel that he'd willingly eat it himself. Who can blame him? It's been found that some of the dog foods, the semimoist ones especially, make an edible hamburger. No horsemeat for Bruno Boy. The hamburger is often beef, better beef than you or I buy at the supermarket. We still have trouble finding hot dogs with much meat in them instead of chicken fat or ground-up bones. However, the Federal Trade Commission guidelines of March 1970 specify that dog food labeled "beef" must contain at least 95 percent of succulent steer. Contrast that with the United States Department of Agriculture regulations for the hot dog you or I munch at the football game. It can have as little as 55 percent real meat, with the rest of the stuffing a baleful aggregate of fat, bone, water, seasoning, and God knows what else. But when it comes to dog food, the department has a voluntary certification program which lets the manufacturer who meets its dog-food standards label the product proudly, "Packed under continuous supervision." Face it: your dog eats better than you do.

77

The fastest growing dog-food lines are often the most expensive. For instance Voila Foods for Pets, my handy calculator tells me, cost over a dollar a pound. Julia Child wouldn't scorn their Beef Burgundy or Kidney Stew. Canine Carriage Trade Corporation pushes a gourmet line featuring Liver Pate and Chicken Continental. Let Bruno Boy gulp down any of these and he'll give a gratifying belch before curling up on your new davenport.

Now let's look at another angle. The United States has yet to take a dog census but one guess is that half a million dogs roam the scruffy streets of our largest city, New York. And help to make them scruffier. The kicker is that not only are there more dogs all the time but bigger ones. A New York *Times* report of a year ago noted a brisk market for Great Danes, St. Bernards, and Newfoundlands, as well as for the German Shepherds which apartment dwellers have long been buying in a frantic search for protection. *Newsweek* last spring estimated the ultimate result: 50,000 tons of dog droppings on the sidewalks and curbs each year. Plus 5 million gallons of urine (this last I must admit strikes me as a wild surmise). The excrement is a health hazard besides being a foul nuisance, for according to the *Times* article it shelters a worm called *toxacara canis* which, if we ingest it, can cause lung disease, brain damage, or blindness.

But the profits are both great and growing. Dog foods find a market among the richest rich and the poorest poor. The latest survey I've seen of the state of the industry, in *Barron's* for March 3, 1969, shows that the sales of canned, dry, and semimoist foods totaled $661,000,000 in 1968. An unofficial estimate shows that in 1970 the sales passed a billion dollars, and 1971 promises to be the most profitable year so far. This when we're experiencing an unemployment rate of 6 percent for the entire country and only a little less for New York itself. And the rise in New York's welfare cases is rocketlike. Back in Bedford-Stuyvesant and Harlem, mothers buy dog food (the cheaper kind, no Liver Pate) for their families to eat. So do some college students, to my personal knowledge. I've been in the kitchen of one commune while a student fried up a couple of Gainesburgers for us. I downed mine bravely. From what I've been told—this is an unsolicited testimonial, as they used to say in the patent-medicine days—both the Black ghetto and the youth ghetto prefer Ken-L Ration or Gravy Train. But nobody really knows.

Anyway, they're all supposed to look tempting on television. They all promise that the owner will no longer have to wheedle his pet to eat. The piece in *Barron's* says one thing I won't forget: that the industry is trying to make owners "feel as though they are feeding a child or family member rather than an animal." Though the commercials cost over $85,000,000 annually, they evidently do their job. So our dogs grow wheezy and fat while men lack work and children go hungry. What can one say about a civilization which pays a billion a year for the privilege of committing a massive nuisance?

Without doubt dogs are a luxury we're going to have to surrender. We can take a lead from Chairman Mao. When the first Old China Hands arrived in Peking with President Nixon's party, they saw several striking improvements. One was the utter absence of the barking curs which had once overrun the city. What Mao had done to eliminate them, the visitors couldn't find out; but it worked. Nevertheless, different nations need different remedies, and so for the United States as a whole, I'd propose a $100 yearly tax on each animal, plus a 25 percent tax on pet foods. That tax to go to the smallest taxing unit within which the owner lived, say his ward or borough.

If this didn't work, the ultimate remedy (forgive me) would be to put the canine population to sleep. "Goodbye, Bruno," I'd call out sadly but firmly. "Goodbye, Alpo, goodbye Ken-L Ration, goodbye Purina Dog Chow. Goodbye *Petfood Industry*, doggiest of trade journals. Goodbye Pet Food Institute, stalwart spokesman for a formerly flourishing industry. Goodbye all."

[*I got the idea for "Chow Time" while visiting Manhattan late in 1971. I did some research at the year's end and the* Evening Sun *printed the column in February 1972. This means that my figures, if not my facts, are out of date. My thesis was serious enough but the* Evening Sun *illustrated the column with an amiably comic cartoon which took the edge off. Anyhow, I'm reprinting the column in the hope that it can provide something to think about.*]

27

The President and the
Persian Essence

In my capacity as park-bench counselor to the political elite, I'm
often asked how to win the next presidential election. Even as
early as this, I find that anxious inquiries multiply. And rightly:
the time to begin is now. In fairness to Democrats and Republi-
cans alike, I believe in giving them all the same answer.

I tell them the way to do it is to ignore issues altogether. Pay
no attention to the issues, I say firmly over puffs of my claymore
pipe. I take the long historical view and tell my park-bench part-
ners about my favorite campaign, the one which ousted the
Democrat Martin Van Buren from the White House in 1840. His
opponent was General William Henry Harrison, a military Whig
who had whupped the Indians at Tippecanoe. Though he had
been beaten by Van Buren in 1836, he went on to win handily in
1840. The secret lay in the fact that he and his supporters never
talked about political issues.

They talked instead about Van Buren. Their gleeful leader was
a congressman from Pennsylvania named Charlie Ogle. In a
series of raucous speeches before the House, he charged that
President Van Buren suffered from delusions of royalty. He had
turned the White House into a palace, carpeted with—said the
congressman meaningfully—Royal Wilton and Imperial Brussels.
Now he craved to adorn its Blue Elliptical Saloon with silk tassels
and satin medallions, with galoon and gimp.

In his several speeches during the spring of 1840, he developed his subject further. He expatiated at one point on the palace furniture. In the tone of a Puritan forced to pronounce a foul word, he told a shocked Congress that the palace was crowded with ottomans, candelabras, and tabourets (which he called "tabby cats"). The pampered president, moving regally among his lush furniture, was lavishing public funds on his person also. There was no reason, Ogle declaimed, why the voter should pay for the president's Concentrated Persian Essence or his Corinthian Oil of Cream. Or for—and here the imagination boggled—his Double Extract of Queen Victoria!

Let him pay rent for the White House, continued the egalitarian Ogle. And let him pay for the gardener on the White House grounds; the presidential salary looked sizable enough. Ogle pointed out the stark contrast between the president's palace and the simple log cabin of General Harrison. The *Congressional Globe* for that time notes that he even eulogized the general's Spartan set of pots and pans. Ogle "gave a description of his furniture and cooking utensils"; they were admirable in their austerity.

The Democrats responded to Ogle's guerrilla attack with the voice of reason. It did nothing but spur Ogle on. Soon even some of his fellow Whigs dissented from his methods. High among them stood the respected Massachusetts congressman, Levi Lincoln. No one ever charged Levi Lincoln with having a sense of humor. He answered Ogle literally, first quoting him and then trying to rebut him. But all anyone remembered was the colorful quotations. Ogle insinuated that Levi Lincoln was under "Palace influence." Lincoln replied indignantly. Then he quoted Ogle as criticizing "certain persons, who, perhaps, were in the habit of visiting the White House, shaking the President's taper fingers, and sipping his wine"; and Levi Lincoln went on to say that the criticism was pure malice. However, no one remembered his denial that he was one of those "certain persons" and everyone remembered the president's "taper fingers." No man with taper fingers ever had a chance for reelection.

In rising wrath, Congressman Lincoln even criticized Ogle personally. Why did Ogle try to deny the president the perquisites of office when Ogle himself had them? Hitting a blow with all the force of a feather duster, Lincoln turned to Ogle on the floor of the house and inquired in his Back Bay accent if Ogle did not have some government stationery in his very room? And "has he no Congressional penknife of costly extravagance at this very moment in his pocket?"

However earnestly Congressman Lincoln rebutted, it made not the smallest difference. That November Van Buren got 60 electoral votes while General Harrison got 234. And when on March 4, 1841, President Harrison gave his inaugural address it was perfectly in keeping. It had references to Greece and Rome and even to the Swiss Republic but not one word about the issues.

28

Some Spirits of '76:
Historical Note, 1972

The hucksters took over the plans for the celebration, all right, but they overreached themselves. By early 1971 they were generating a classic reaction. The turning point came in late spring 1972 and the turnaround was a work of folk art.

Feisty old Sam Adams would have been gladdened, I'm sure. His hard gray eye would have gleamed and a sharktooth grin would have split his face. The American Revolution Bicentennial Commission would merely have made him snort but in the People's Bicentennial Commission he would have recognized his kind of folks.

In the best polemical tradition the counter-commission commenced by accusing the ARBC (forgive the initials but we're tight for space) of being a clutch of Tories, all with double chins, fatuous expressions, and an itch for selling Uncle Sam by the pound. The counter-commission leaders were a brace of brash young intellectuals, who rate at least a footnote in all this history. The director was one Jeremy Rifkin, pamphleteering author of "Will the Revolution Succeed?"; and Ed Schwartz, ex-president of the National Student Association, was action coordinator.

The counter-commission soon fastened its gimlet look on such proposals to the ARBC as a Giant Roll of paper with 7 million signatures of Americans willing to stand up and be counted. The idea, according to the outside hucksters offering it to the inside hucksters, was to haul the Giant Roll around among America's 100 most important shopping centers. What better place to find mid-Americans willing to stand up and be counted?

Busting with zeal the counter-commission issued a counter-pamphlet *The Bicentennial Era*, appropriating for it the colors red, white, and blue. In it the counter-commission charged the ARBC with plans to tie in the American Revolution with "such diverse enterprises as the Orange Bowl Parade, the Ringling Brothers Barnum and Bailey Circus, the Miss America Contest, and the McDonald hamburger chain."

I'd been sent a copy of the pamphlet and my mind gawped as I read of these patriotic notions. I could see Bert Parks at the Miss America Contest prancing before the television cameras, dressed as Uncle Sam and mangling a medley of "God Bless America" and "A Pretty Girl is Like a Melody." The opportunities for Ronald McDonald looked just as groovy. I could see him laughing up the Boston Tea Party by dunking a hamburger in his cup or crunching on the saucer with his strong white teeth.

To celebrate America's two hundredth birthday, *The Bicentennial Era* averred further, the big-business bakers of Sara Lee cakes had offered (surprise) to bake the country's Official Cake for the president to cut. Sara Lee had likewise volunteered to bake mini-cakes and merchandise them to patriotic, or at least hungry, citizens.

If you've got cake you need ice cream. The makers of Baskin-Robbins's myriad flavors promptly stood up to be counted too. They announced that they were ready to produce "a great American ice cream series . . . the Betsy Ross Twirl—red, white, and blue; the George Washington Cherry Tree, etc." Also you need birthday cards for the nation's two hundredth birthday. The Hallmark Company announced that it would soon be marketing cards distinguished by their patriotism, quaintness, and "wholesome humor about the New Spirit of '76." In passing I should note that to my regret they haven't appeared; I can scarcely wait to see the wholesome fun made of the new spirit of '76.

The nation's communities seemed as eager and full of ideas as the nation's companies, said *The Bicentennial Era*. California's communities of course led them all. In Mariposa, for instance, the DAR proposed to raise a fresh flagpole; the town promised to see to it that its old cemeteries were "located, cataloged, and cleaned up." Bakersfield volunteered to publish a booklet with seventy-six reasons why America was great. Hollywood promised to award a special Bicentennial Oscar.

The East Coast as well was busy, it appeared. In Boston there were plans to paint all the commuter buses red, white, and you-know-what. In Washington the horn of plenty was going to pour its contents all over the national capital. *The Bicentennial Era* singled out two projects for special mention: a huge Federal Bicentennial Exhibit in the Great Hall of the Commerce Department, on the triumphs of American business, and the Eisenhower Sports and Convention Center planned for downtown Washington.

Despite this untimely exposure of plans and proposals the ARBC announced, biting its lip, that it was pressing right on. Yet it didn't. The picture of Paul Revere riding in his Mercedes to rouse the countryside somehow had less and less appeal. The counter-commission did better, actually accomplishing part of its own celebration. But all in all the Bicentennial never got the good handling it deserved. They ran the ARBC up the flagpole, Dick, but it didn't fly.

29

Reviving Henry

The great books of the past, we like to think, have been selected for us by a system as infallible as any pope. The Test of Time, we say with reverence, has separated the rare grains of literary wheat from the tons of chaff. . . . Not so.

There are literary fads and fashions as whimsical as any created by the dress designers of London, Paris, or New York. In the two fields I work in oftenest, mid-nineteenth- and early-twentieth-century American literature, I watch the changes with open-mouthed interest. Right now, the writer I appreciate most, Henry David Thoreau, is slipping slightly. His brand of individualism and social (or antisocial) action is losing at least a fraction of its appeal. On the other hand, Ralph Waldo Emerson is coming up. His individualism is gnomic, withdrawn. His nearly oriental passivity and his interest in the scriptures of the East speak directly to those of my students who respond to the attractions of Zen or who find in pot the key to what I might call innerness.

In early twentieth-century literature, F. Scott Fitzgerald was out of fashion for a decade after his death. His writing came to be considered flashy; his scale of values, it was agreed, was suitable for a highschool senior. Then a slow rise started. Today anything he wrote, no matter how juvenile, how trivial, can find not only a publisher but respectful readers. As a matter of fact the whole decade of the 1920s, when Fitzgerald flourished, is once again the basis for a mode. Our clothes, furniture, films, and art now have a tinge of the twenties to them.

But H. L. Mencken, the last of the famous writers of that decade to renew his appeal, is having a harder time. Somehow, in spite of his fabulous wit, his own trenchant individualism, and his central position during the decade itself, he isn't being read as much as I for one believe he deserves. Partly this is because some of his ideas and attitudes currently repel us: his elitism, for instance, his pro-Germanism, his loud opposition to the welfare state. But it's partly because of simple bad luck. For example, the abortive attempt to stage an "Evening with Mencken" in the vein of the highly successful evenings with Mark Twain, with Hal Holbrook impersonating Twain, and Charles Dickens, with Emlyn Williams impersonating Dickens.

Not long ago the "Evening" was staged at Ford's Theater in Washington, with the veteran actor David Wayne playing Mencken. If Mencken had had his way, he would sooner have appeared on Baltimore's Charles Street in his BVDs. Wayne's impersonation was, to use one of Mencken's wonted terms, plausible enough. The stance, flat-footed; the mannerisms, including the contemplation of the stogie; the gravelly Baltimore accent: all these carried an air of conviction to most of the audience, myself among them. Whether they did to the few old-timers who knew him personally, I couldn't say; but to us youngsters who admired him but never shook his hand, they added up to a quite likely Mencken.

Yet there was something off-putting about seeing him on the stage. He turned wooden, unnatural. The show faltered and in a few weeks failed. Holbrook could revive Mark Twain in such a masterly manner partly because Mark was always giving public lectures and so his being center-stage looked natural. Similarly Williams could revive Charles Dickens the more realistically because Dickens was always giving public readings from his works. In fact Williams used a replica of the odd, one-armed lectern Dickens employed.

Mencken, however, in actual life proved nearly impossible to lure to the public platform. For fifteen years one of America's leading lecture bureaus offered him up to $5,000 for a relatively short series of winter engagements. For fifteen years he said, Thank you, no. True, he would sometimes talk to college students here or there but only in an atmosphere of discursive informality. Only at Goucher College did he allow himself an annual appearance. This was a tribute to the persuasive powers of a friend on the Goucher faculty, Professor Harry Baker. It was in April 1923, that he first enticed Mencken to address the young ladies of the college on "The Trade of Letters."

The most illuminating thing is that when Mencken reached the rostrum he surveyed the "two hundred and fifty virgins" (his description) before him and then shoved his notes back into his pocket. Instead of speechifying he talked at them like a stand-up comedian, high-level of course, on how to catch a husband. By one of the nice ironies of history Sara Haardt sat in the audience and Sara Haardt ultimately caught Mencken himself.

Goucher could count itself blest. The 1920s were Mencken's peak period; his vogue on college campuses was colossal. If you merged the best points of Norman Mailer and William Buckley, threw in the literary quixotism of Leslie Fiedler, and seasoned it with the sardonic humor of Dick Gregory, you'd have some idea of what the college students of the 1920s saw in him. He seemed such a skyrocket that Midwestern university facilities quailed at inviting him. The East Coast institutions showed more daring. Again and again Mencken felt forced to say no to bids from Yale, Columbia, Dartmouth, and other eminent—if slightly esoteric— institutions.

A few times, though, he yielded to the enticement of faculty friends. He would talk, but never lecture, he promised Billy Phelps of Yale at one point. Talk he did, with all the wit and brash charm that permeated his polemics in the *Evening Sun* and *American Mercury*. Although he admitted in more than one private letter that he didn't care for college students, the myth spread throughout the campuses that he was a sophomore at heart. The result was that if he'd wanted to become a performing seal on ivy-festooned platforms, he could have doubled his income. He needed no lecture bureau; his reputation was enough.

That is, until the Great Depression arrived in 1929 and began pounding American values into new and strange shapes. Then the students tossed him aside and turned to Mike Gold. Network radio, however, was booming and in the 1930s he did some broadcasts for NBC. An NBC photographer snapped several pictures of him; he later pronounced one of them his pet likeness.

Television arrived too late for him. It was just developing into a national phenomenon when he suffered his crippling stroke of 1948. He would have squirmed at the talk shows, I suspect, with their relentless exploitation of personality. He would have been outraged by the commercials coming every seven minutes. Still, if a Harry Baker or Billy Phelps happened to be around to persuade him, we might have the pleasure of an occasional appearance. Or maybe of only one appearance. I can see him trampling all over television's taboos with boots covered by Baltimore's red clay.

"Mr. Mencken, Hank baby," the toothy talk-show host might say, "could we have your opinion on a few things? Let's start, ha ha, with love."

Love? "Love is the delusion that one woman differs from another."

Democracy? "The theory that the common people know what they want, and deserve to get it good and hard."

Conscience? "The inner voice that warns us someone may be looking."

The American farmer? "No more grasping, selfish and dishonest mammal is known to students of Anthropoidea."

Remorse? "Regret that one waited so long to do it."

. . . "Well, folks, time for a fast commercial for Zippo Soap to, ha ha, wash our mouths out."

30

Penning Poems for
Fun and Profit

The poet-laureate business simply isn't what it used to be. I believe that the poet laureate of England still gets a ruddy royal parchment, plus a yearly hogshead of English malt. The poet laureate of all Maryland gets a $500 expense account. But you can't live on malt and parchment nor on a grungy $500 a year.

Notwithstanding, we'll probably always have poet laureates (or poets laureate?). It's just that there are fewer of them now. Once even Baltimore boasted a poet laureate—one of my favorite bad poets in fact. He was "Professor" Alexander Geddes, nicknamed "Eck," a longtime friend and suppliant of H. L. Mencken.

A reedy Scot, he showed an incurable craving for the limelight, from his flashy youth to his tottering old age. Early in our century he acted at Baltimore's Hollywood Park, being billed in large electric letters as "Professor Alexander, the Star of Hollywood Park." He went on to produce shows there, in partnership with one Oliver Ziegfeld. One night his political enemies—even poets have them—invaded the hall where he was starring as well as co-producing the show. Forewarned, he did his turn on the stage with a beefy policeman on each side of him, a policeman standing in either wing, and several policemen stationed in the peanut gallery. This shook the audience. As his sister recalled in a letter to Mencken, "Women were crying all over the house, but the show went on." Directly after it ended, Eck shoved his share of the proceeds in his shoe and hotfooted it for home.

When he wasn't cavorting on the stage, he was writing at his desk. He did squibs and stories for the Baltimore *Herald* when Mencken was its boy editor. He stood ready to do poetry also but Mencken wasn't buying that—he had poetry of his own he wished to print. Yet Eck was determined. After several years he started to sell a few verses. Or as his sister put it, he "began to commercial his talent for writing poetry." He broke into the *Sun*, which every Baltimorean read from birth, and shortly afterward scrambled up the side of Parnassus.

It was Mayor Thomas Preston who designated him "Poet Laureate of Baltimore." The ceremony took place at City Hall. Eck read a poem, composed for the occasion and breathtakingly exact in rhyme and rhythm. His cup, he is reported to have declaimed, was full to overflowing. But only metaphorically, for the problem was that poetry still didn't seem to pay. That is, until Eck elected to force it.

He did so by penning poems each year for religious high-holidays, posting them to his acquaintances, and petitioning for a bit of cash in return. At this he kept on for thirty years. Though we don't have most of his missives to Mencken, we have copies of Mencken's replies at the Enoch Pratt Library. Here is an extract from one of Mencken's letters of 1932: "If I were rich I'd send you a check for $100,000 but, unfortunately, I am suffering, like the rest of humanity, from the Hoover horrors." A year later: "The best I can do for the moment is the enclosed." Four years later: "I am enclosing a small check against the cost of your Christmas broadside." And so on.

Eck customarily composed an Easter broadside as well as a Christmas one every year. Though the cash returns from the Easter hymns were doubtless modest, the Christmas jingles evidently did much better. They were lyrics of plum-pudding sentimentality, usually devoted to the twin topics of Santa Claus and good cheer.

The broadside for Christmas 1938 survives. It carries eight poems, all of unblemished badness. They reveal an Eck who always had to tussle with the English language but never let it pin him. Following the poems, Eck prints Christmas greetings to, guilefully, a pair of tycoons of the steel business Charles M. Schwab and Eugene Grace and to an eminent Rhode Island couple Mr. and Mrs. John Nicholas Brown. At the end he addresses his public: "I hope those who receive a copy of my *Christmas Bells* may respond through an offering. . . ."

I have space for only one of the stanzas from the 1938 broadside but I freely confess that I regard it as superlative. It's the final stanza of "Santa's Coming." In it Eck summons all his art to write:

> *Dear old Christmas! tis so sweet,*
> *For young and old it is a treat;*
> *And may we still be children yet*
> *To never Santa Claus forget.*

31

Flex Those Muscles, Stem That Sternum

I once knew a man who got to be Mayor of Milwaukee. I know how he stayed in office. Whenever he had to make conversation with some voter, he'd ask solicitously, "How's the old complaint?" The dam would open, and the voter would pour out the tale of his constant cough or his lumbago or his sensitive stomach.

I suppose most of us are hagridden by our old complaint. The search for abounding health must be eternal. Certainly it's been an American obsession. Over the decades the message has remained much the same but the style has changed delightfully. You see it best when you set the old next door to the new. A glossy example of the old is *Vitality Supreme*, a book by Bernarr ("Muscles") MacFadden first printed in 1915. A flourishing example of the new is *Aerobics* by Kenneth Cooper, M.D., copyright 1968. Its cover brags, "Over 1,250,000 Copies in Print!! The Exercise Program for Men and Women that has Changed the Lives of Millions of Americans." And it's still selling like $1.95 beefsteak.

Dr. Cooper's style is punchy, with short paragraphs and scrappy sentences. He talks to you direct, breathing healthily in your face. You can do it, he urges; you can follow the Cooper plan. And if you do, the sky is the limit. What happened to others who did it? They improved their personalities as well as their physiques. They shucked off anxiety and learned to relax. "They had a better self-image and more confidence in themselves."

What you do is to measure your regular exercise on a point scale so that you don't have too little or, for that matter, too much. Dr. Cooper's main contribution lies in his disclosure that it doesn't have to be strenuous exercise. You don't need to bust a gut. Running, swimming, bicycling, and walking are his favorites —and the running doesn't need to be swift. He offers us a vivid picture of his wife Millie running: "After she gets me off to work, she puts the baby in a stroller and our dog on a leash and pushing one and dragging the other, she runs through the streets of our suburban neighborhood."

But it takes more than Millie or her husband the doctor to match Bernarr MacFadden. He writes with an evangelical wallop. "Why not," he demands, "throb with superior vitality? Why not possess the physical strength of a young lion?" Like the doctor he promises enticing rewards. They are more than merely a bulging biceps; they are "a magnificent harvest of physical, mental and spiritual attainments." His method is Show and Tell. He laces his book with photos of Bernarr in action and Bernarr in repose. The first one portrays him standing nobly erect, though in a suit obviously ordered by mail from Hong Kong. The second one shows him, still baggy-suited, sitting in a chair whose hind legs are four inches short. Why? It helps you "in fighting for a straight spine."

The next series reveals him, now dressed only in what looks like a cummerbund, rippling his muscles as he does his evolutions. He presses his neck to exercise his thyroid gland. He pushes himself up on his brawny fingertips and toes for his thorax's sake. He laughs as an exercise, directing us to "Stand with the feet wide apart and then bring the hands down with a vigorous slap just above the knees as shown in the central photograph. Now bring the bent arms upward and outward at the sides . . . and proceed to make a noise as nearly like a laugh as possible." Ha Ha!

Though we see his wife (girl friend?) less often, two photos of her are unforgettable. One shows her exercising her teeth. I challenge you to guess how she exercises her teeth! The other shows her exercising her inner organs, with her fist clenched against her sternum in the TV comic's familiar gesture of heartburn.

The text itself proves to be mainly flat-footed prescription but with an infusion of revivalist rhetoric. A typical prescription: "If your teeth are decayed the offending members should be removed or the cavities filled." A typical flower of rhetoric: "If the day is gloomy, if the sun is obscured by clouds, then develop the sunshine in your own spirit."

However, I must admit that one blends so well with the other that it's usually hard to separate them. Here, in varying proportions, are a few of the quotations from *Vitality Supreme* which I savor most; all have Cultural Significance. For one: "Wheat, as produced by the Almighty, is practically a perfect food." For another: "Air baths are valuable." Incidentally, you yourself can enjoy an air bath while you sleep, by rigging a clothes line between your 1915-style bedposts and pinning a blanket to it to make a tent. Finally: "Sing at every opportunity" and "A few minutes of singing before each meal would enable one to digest his food far more satisfactorily."

The life styles of *Aerobics* and *Vitality Supreme* look light-years apart. Yet they are tied together at the base. For both are founded on the assumption—so touching, so American—that by an act of will we can make ourselves better. We are not the creatures of environment, the toys of heredity, but self-energizing human beings. I don't know that I agree fully but I find that assumption far more congenial than its opposite. Up Cooper, up MacFadden! I say.

32

Inside the American Driver; or, Ambivalent about Amber

Dear Jeremy:

I'm happy that you're finally coming over, now that your Oxford years have ended. I'm confident you'll enjoy your American visit and will need little guidance about it. With one exception. The use of the automobile is one of the pivotal points of American life, so I'd better tell you a few things about it that you'll never read in the London *Times* or see in the newest movie about Manhattan.

I've been (as you will be) a pedestrian, a passenger, and a driver. The observations I can offer are the hard-bought fruit of experience. I can show you some of the scars, mental and physical.

Let me begin by noting that no American driver obeys the posted speed limits. On the other hand he's not flagrantly disobedient either. Our custom is to drive from five to ten miles above the posted limit. A sixty-mile limit on the Beltway keeps the ordinary driver down to seventy, a seventy-mile limit down to perhaps seventy-eight, and so on. The rare times when the penalty for speeding is exacted come after an accident.

No driver obeys Stop signs either. We employ instead what we call the "sliding stop," really a glissade. However, when we reach a Stop-and-Go signal, we do stop if the light shows red. Even at four in the morning. More than once I've sat frozen before a red at that glum hour though I couldn't spot another pair of headlights for blocks around. Most of us are ambivalent about amber, I should add. We often try to beat the amber light. (Are you following this? It may seem trivial to you today but it may save your life later.)

Parking violations are like roulette. You never know when your number will come up. It's a sensible idea, though, not to be guilty of the grossest violations. Incidentally, when you park overtime at a metered space, you don't have to put in another nickel or dime if you're not caught. Just count it your good fortune that you haven't been ticketed.

If you're ever in dire need of a parking space, double-park at the most convenient spot and then simply raise the hood of your car. Everyone will respect this distress signal. When you return, lower the hood and drive off. If anybody chances to be watching, pause for a moment first and peer at your engine in puzzlement.

Now I'm going to say a bit about two groups of motorists you'll meet with great frequency, truck drivers and taxi drivers. Though I recognize that every generalization about a group is suspect, I wouldn't be doing my duty if I shunned the subject.

It's a tenet of the American creed that truck drivers are Good Samaritans, endearingly helpful in their gruff way to the motorist in trouble. Some are. But there is a vengeful minority who act instead like paranoid bullies. They drive a vehicle so big that no motorist can compete with it. They break most if not all of the speed regulations. They not only double-park but triple-park. Yet I've never seen a truck driver arrested by a policeman; they seem to be above the law. Truck drivers on the highway are a still bloodier menace than truck drivers on the city street. I read of a Senate hearing recently where it was testified that most long-haul drivers use pep pills to stay awake and keep to the swift schedules that the greedy owners set up for them. When you see a huge diesel coming at you out of the night, you would do well to mutter an Anglican prayer.

Cab drivers are like policemen. Their good nature is constantly eroded by the abrasions of life, specifically the abrasions of traffic. They may set out loving the human race; they end by regarding it at best with dour dislike and at worst with foaming hostility. Most of them can't compare with your London cab drivers in competence. But I ought to add that my personal experience with them has been all right.

Cab drivers are often manic misanthropes. Truck drivers are often highway bullies. Teen-age males—I haven't mentioned them before—are often such reckless show-offs that their insurance rates run double those of teen-age females. Female drivers of any age are often believed by males to be whimsical beyond imagining. Yet there is one other set of drivers I regard as so menacing that I must warn you earnestly against them. These are the old men with hats. Beware, Jeremy, beware. When you see an old man, felt hat settled squarely on his head, driving in the middle of the road at thirty miles an hour, slow up and slip into a side street. It's the only way to escape a broken bumper or pleated fender on your trusty Triumph.

But I mustn't be guilty of sexual inequity. I should cite one other menace: the little old lady, also wearing a hat, sitting on three pillows to let her see over the steering wheel and with eyes staring straight ahead with never a glance at the rear-view mirror. She drives an unexpected forty miles an hour. When you see her ahead of you, make a U-turn even if it's illegal and drive the other way, fast.

I share these insights with you without apology. American drivers are a desperate lot but so are your otherwise considerate countrymen. Italian drivers are an abomination. German drivers are besotted by speed. You can add your own examples. I finish by reminding you that it's always the drivers from another country who drive the worst. I stood two years ago on a street in Belgrade with a Yugoslav friend; a car roared by and my friend swore, "Those damn Greek drivers!"

33

Lament for W. Witkowski

So long, Walter Witkowski!

It all happened so fast. The papers reported that the milkmen's union was striking Daley's Dairy and two others. That was just last week, and yesterday Daley's announced that they were going out of business. I think you and your union brothers were booby-trapped, Walter. Today we got our final bill, not from you but mailed from their office—by computer. I guess we won't be seeing you again.

The whole thing had an air of indecent haste to it. Like that scruffy Kansas railroad which was allowed, a while back, to cancel a run and so simply shoved off the passengers at a junction to nowhere. You and I didn't even have a chance to talk about the strike.

I enjoyed our conversations, I want to add. My house stood near the end of your route. You'd stop sometimes if I was working on my lawn, and once we'd agreed about the weather and properly defined its current condition, you'd bring up at least one unanswerable question. Then we'd ventilate it.

One of your favorites was: "Doc, why do these college kids raise so much hell? Don't they know they've got it made?" I had no push-button answer but we'd worry the question a while anyhow.

Another favorite: "Doc, how come this country gets deeper in debt every year and still keeps going?" Walter, I don't have an answer to that one either. I'm not sure that Daley's does, for that matter. Nor do you.

And I worry about you because, all hokum aside, you stand for something good in this country that we're losing. You're a classic example of the blue-collar worker, one of whose marks is that he hasn't worn a blue collar for years. The street people or the militants may run around in a blue shirt with a blue collar, but not you. You wore a corduroy jacket and a plaid flannel shirt in winter and a Hawaiian sports shirt, tail flapping, in summer. You believed in hard work and reliability—I can't recall a day when you didn't deliver that quart of milk and pint of half & half. You set them carefully in the tin box on our back steps and in hot weather you dropped some crushed ice around them.

What'll I do now? Well, it'll be one more heavy thing to lug home from the supermarket . . . The supermarket, where I always pick the slowest line to put my cart in . . . The supermarket, where I stare at the cabalistic figures on the cartons of milk and feel sure every time that I'm picking out the most ancient carton. Is there three-day-old cream on the shelf at Jumbo-Gigantic? That's the cream I pick. It's sour by the next morning.

So you're disappearing, without fuss but to our considerable loss. I would have been willing to pay a couple of cents more to have my milk delivered. Moreover, to me you stand not only for the vanishing blue-collar worker but for a whole side of American life which is quietly dropping into limbo. I can think of lots of examples, mechanical as well as human. You know from our talks that the running-board is one of my favorites. This, boys and girls, was a shelf on each side of the automobile which let you step up and into it. It was more convenient by a country mile than our present design without running-boards, which makes us squat down into the front or back seat instead of stepping up with dignity. And if you think getting in is hard for some of us, wait till you see some of us getting out. It's real work for a fat lady, for instance, to shoehorn into a Ford Pinto. Or even into a puffed-up Buick. But when she has to get out—. All modesty is abandoned while she tries to raise her 200 pounds and thrust them out of the automobile. Sometimes she looks up helplessly at you, wedged as she is between the doorposts. She's made it off the cushioned seat but she'll never make it the rest of the way without a shot of TNT to boost her.

And a human example of something now in limbo? I offer you the scissors-grinder. He used to come around in his panel truck each spring and summer. "Shears! Mowers! Shears! Mowers!" That was his professional cry. You could hear it blocks away, especially the long-drawn-out "Mowwerrrsss!" Now who's going to add an edge to my lawn mower or sharpen our assemblage of household scissors? We'll have to haul them all to Mitvack's Hardware, in the Shopping Center, and leave them there for two weeks. They'll come back to us a bit sharper but with an added tariff of time, trouble, and money.

Of course I don't want to push sentiment too far, The Oldest Inhabitants have told me that they still remember the call "OOO EEE AAA!" That stood for "Odorless Excavating Apparatus." The call came from the privy-cleaners who rode up and down the alleys till shortly after World War I, offering their useful if inglorious services. I confess that I prefer current plumbing, even though it costs as much as a doctor's house call to bring in a plumber. (But I forget: doctors don't make house calls anymore.)

Regardless, I lament the loss of the milkman and his friends. I'll miss you, Walter. I hope that you find another, and equally good, job and that there isn't even a ripple in the Witkowski family economy. Because I'm afraid you and I aren't like the United States Government. We can't live on deficit spending. I'd like to send you a card on Christmas, at least, but I don't even know where you live. So—so long, Walter Witkowski, wherever you are, out there.

34

White House Sit-In

Nature copies Art, all right. And in my limited purview seldom improves on it.

My supporting witness at this point is the late great William Faulkner, who was able to provide Nature with a thought-provoking and indeed prophetic model.

Let me, with a dramatic flourish, pull from the books at the back of my desk the *Collected Stories of William Faulkner* and open it to a story entitled "Lo!" He wrote it more than forty years ago, in 1933 to be precise, but it's as timely as today. For it's about a sit-in at the White House, not by college militants nor ghetto Blacks but by Indians.

The story starts with the president, who roughly resembles Andrew Jackson, about to steal out from the White House at 6:30 on a winter morning in an era roughly like Jackson's. He opens the door of his dressing room a crack. He sees, "lying upon the deep, rich pile of the corridor carpet, a bone. It was a cooked bone, a rib; to it still adhered close shreds of flesh holding in neat and overlapping halfmoons the marks of human teeth."

The teeth belong to a covey of Indian braves camped outside in the corridor. They have squatted there three weeks waiting, under their chief Frank Weddel, for justice—and justice with a certain pomp—from the president. A white man had tricked them into selling the only ford for 300 miles across their stream and then had tried to charge them for crossing. Weddel's young nephew had split the fellow's skull. Now Weddel and his tribe want a proper trial for the boy, and the ford returned. So they have come to the great chief in his white house.

This morning the president successfully slips away to the home of his secretary of the interior. There the two men decide to rush through a makeshift ceremony, declare the nephew innocent, and persuade the Indians to go back to their lands beyond the Mississippi. The Indians are summoned, watch the hasty doings impassively, and are far from impressed.

Weddel explains blandly, "In my ignorance I had thought that even our little affair would have been concluded in" the Capitol. But it hadn't been, and so he and his braves will wait. In the White House. In fact more Indians are coming to join them in the waiting.

"And so it was," says Faulkner, "that up that Avenue with a high destiny the cavalcade moved in the still falling snow, led by the carriage containing the President and the uncle and nephew . . .: so it was that behind the Speaker's desk . . . the President and the Secretary stood, while below them . . . the uncle and nephew stood, with behind them the dark throng of kin and friends and acquaintances."

This time the president gives them the full treatment. They hear his sonorous voice reading to them in an exotic tongue; the Indians have no way of knowing that he is reading the Latin text of ten of Petrarch's sonnets from a book the secretary has snatched along for him. Then the president drops his arm, and outside the crash of ceremonial artillery is heard as he has ordered. At this, even the Indians stir with a murmur of pleased astonishment. The president announces, now in sonorous English, that the nephew is free.

The treatment works. But one thing remains. As Frank Weddel reminds the president politely, "And now, about the little matter of the cursed ford . . ." The upshot is an executive order that the ford shall belong to the Indians in perpetuity—as long as they never come east again.

I've thought about this story more than once. I thought about it when the poor, black and white, were building Resurrection City (remember?) almost within earshot of the White House. I thought about it later when Indians occupied the Bureau of Indian Affairs less than a mile further off. And, I must say, I'm thinking about it now: I wonder what else Faulkner has predicted?

35

Secrets of Treating
the Young

Mrs. H. O. writes distractedly from Brighton, England. "Dear Mr. Bode, I've just seen your letter in the *Times* on the younger generation. My husband and I have a daughter in our local comprehensive school and a son at the University of Sussex. Both have string hair and no manners. Our daughter refuses to speak to us. Our son speaks to us all the time but whatever we reply is wrong. Please help."

And, in Maryland, from Ruxton: "Why won't my Sandra wash? I turn on the TV commercials constantly, yet she just curls her lip."

From Frostburg: "Lawrence says he's getting stoned every week but I don't see any bruises."

From Rising Sun: "Our daughter Jerri, who is a sophomore at Maryland, tells us that she's doing a lot of intervisitation. Every time she comes home she does nothing except flop on her bed and sleep."

From Baltimore County: "Why do they wear bluejeans and elf-boots? Why do they get mad when you talk to them? How can we deal with them?"

How can we deal with them? Dear friends, I'm touched that you think I can tell you just because I teach college students. Yet

I do have a recipe which I myself have found imperfect but useful.

I treat them like Hindus.

I treat them as if they belonged to a different culture from our own. I begin by frankly conceding the differences but not pre-judging either their culture or ours. I tolerate their touchy sense of caste and their curious caste marks. Their wristbands, the fringed purses that both the young women and the young men carry on campus, the bare feet, the fatigue jackets, the golliwog walk. I admire the utility of their uniform, which rarely requires changing and which can be shucked off or slipped on anywhere. I regret their hostility to those outside their caste, especially the Untouchables: the booming businessman and his busty wife.

I defer to their most venerated religion, astrology. I myself await the wonders of the Age of Aquarius. When some sopho-more assures me that he blew Friday's quiz because of a bad cusp, I nod my head in simulated sympathy. When another student asks for my birth date, I recognize that she doesn't hope to bribe me with a birthday present. She simply wants to find a clue to her teacher's disposition. By the way, students, I'm a Pisces. Sorry about that.

I comply with their customs. They would rather sit than stand, rather lounge than sit upright, and rather lie down than lounge. So when they and I talk (they quit saying "rap" the day Madison Avenue started to), I lie back on my chair and survey the beige ceiling. A helpful minor point: never look them is the eye when talking. It makes them skittish.

I respect their basic mode. When they retire to their interiors, when they smoke pot for a "wise passivity" (ah, Emerson), when they sit alone in Zen—when they do these things they are reacting against our own feverish, salesmanlike, aggressive cul-ture. Who wants to be the chief used-car dealer in Hyattsville? Who wants to be the milky mother of a brood of six? Not my students.

I think I understand one of the itchiest resentments, the re-sentment against receiving. We've always given them everything we can, particularly everything we can buy. We have constantly forced gifts on them. Remember, parents, that it's still harder to receive than give. When I lived in London a pretty Hindu girl asked me, "Mr. Bode, why can't you Americans learn to give gracefully?" I answered firmly though not tartly.

Which brings me to my final suggestion. Don't be overpolite just because you realize the difference in cultures. Don't be mealy-mouthed. The young will consider that you are condescending to them and will despise you for it.

If you carry out my suggestions I predict that your relations with the young will become as harmonious as our country's with Hindustan.

That'll be $50, please.

36

Bayard Taylor's
Bad Trip—And Ours

"The walls of my frame were burst outward and tumbled into ruin. . . . I felt that I existed through a vast extent of space. . . . Before me—for a thousand leagues, as it seemed—stretched a vista of rainbows, whose colors gleamed with the splendor of gems—arches of living amethyst, sapphire, emerald, topaz, and ruby. By thousands and tens of thousands, they flew past me, as my dazzling barge sped down the magnificent arcade; yet the vista still stretched as far as ever before me. . . . The Spirits of Light, Color, Odor, Sound, and Motion were my slaves; and, having these, I was master of the universe."

The psychedelic scene near the end of the movie *2001*? No. That was Bayard Taylor, writing in 1855 in his book *The Lands of the Saracen*, on how it felt to take hash. In his day, before the Civil War, he was the prince of American travel writers. He made a lush living out of journeying to far places and then lecturing and writing about it. By the time he published *The Lands of the Saracen* he stood at the peak of his reputation. He lectured from Boston to Baltimore, from Philadelphia to Chicago. He perfected a routine especially aimed at the ladies who flocked to listen to him. We have several drawings of him in Arab dress on the lecture platform. In one he turns his head, his heavy-lidded eyes brooding beneath his turban, his nostrils arched, his beard and mustachioes a-curl. His hand lies on his scimitar, ready to draw. Small wonder housewives swooned.

A highlight of his excursion to the Middle East was the experience he later wove into a chapter called "The Visions of Hasheesh." It must have made his audiences both thrill and tremble. For after describing his vision of the "vista of rainbows" he showed how his hash trip turned bad. He became "a mass of transparent jelly, and a confectioner poured me into a twisted mold. I threw my chair aside, and writhed and tortured myself. . . . I threw myself on my bed, with the excited blood still roaring wildly in my ears, my heart throbbing with a force that seemed to be rapidly wearing away my life, my throat dry as a potsherd, and my stiffened tongue cleaving to the roof of my mouth—resisting no longer, but awaiting my fate with the apathy of despair."

I realize that many of my students know more about all this than I do. In fact they don't hesitate to tell me so, at some length. I can understand their impulse to smoke pot better after reading Bayard Taylor. And I see that they have an argument to support the impulse. I think they are unwise to use pot, let alone experiment with anything stronger, yet I feel that their argument shouldn't be ignored. Without a doubt pot and other anodynes are on their way to being completely legal; even if we don't look at them they won't go away.

Here is how the argument runs (I hear it often in my line of work). My students start with an attack on alcohol. Look, they say, drinking is the curse of your generation. You invented Alcoholics Anonymous and you certainly needed to. Drink messes up the senses and hurts the judgment. It kills thousands of people on the highways each year. Basically it does nothing but brutalize. But notice how your culture regards it. For you there's nothing cuter than a drunk. He's the standard source of comedy. He staggers and reels, making funny faces and mumbling funny things. The most classic of your comedians, old Jackie Gleason or Red Skelton for example, would be lost without their drunk routines. The second stringers, from Dean Martin back to Phil Harris, use liquor as a comedy prop. Depicting a drunk draws as surefire applause as coming from Brooklyn or being Irish. You're fantastically indulgent toward alcohol.

So why scream, they continue, when we smoke pot? Nobody on pot ever hurt anybody else. We don't even make a nuisance of ourselves, as drunks do. We're quiet, withdrawn. We leave a world made up of drunks (or how do you explain Vietnam or Watergate) for contemplation, for visions, for deep sense experience. What if the trips sometimes go wrong? We don't lose control of ourselves; we actually learn to increase our control.

My answer to them is succinct: alcohol as a rule leads to little except more alcohol. Marijuana apparently leads to harder drugs, including LSD and heroin. I try to add, if they're still listening, that we haven't seen nearly enough research even on pot to prove that the effects are not permanently damaging.

Bayard Taylor? I've looked into his life and, so far as I can find out, he never tried hash again. I wonder if he took to drink?

37

The Name Game

Are you happy with your name? Head hanging, I admit I'm not with mine. It has been years since I fantasized during the middle of the night about what I really should have been called, but even today I consider that my parents could have done better. Much better. "A short first name to go with a short last one," my father once told me in the accents of a major oracle, while I thought wistfully of a name like Wellington Koo. Wellington Koo was the Chinese ambassador to the United States during the Pastoral Age; he wore the name with enormous panache. Or, in a different vein, a name like C. K. Dexter Havens, which was inspired as I remember it by seeing Cary Grant play the character called that in *The Philadelphia Story*. Or, to sail back to the other end of the spectrum to simplicity, "Mike" something or other. What a good, no-nonsense name, respected by the boys in the block for its honest male aura!

There are many names besides mine which I don't admire, and some must have been a heavy burden to the bearer. Think of the old Puritans. Among the names their parents gave them and which caught H. L. Mencken's attention in *The American Language* were Fear-Not, Increase, and Fly-Fornication.

A fair share of the young people I know, particularly the college students, pronounce themselves, when asked, unhappy

111

about their names also. If they're black they tend to look to Africa when renaming themselves. A young woman may call herself Misonu, Effua, or Younousea, for example. A young man may pick Imari, say, or Karamu or Gaidi. They wear their new names as they wear their Afro: it furnishes them with a fresh identity. If the name happens to have a royal sound to it, there's nothing wrong with that. A generation ago kingly names were all too rare among Blacks. I recall only one though it was magnificent: H. R. Hammurabi Robb.

If my students are Jewish they look to Israel, though not as much as the Blacks look to Africa. The young men favor emphatically Old Testament names such as Jonathan or Joel as well as those with a kibbutz flavor added such as Uri or Amiram. The young women seem to pick names like Deborah or Tamar, Ilana or Aliza. There are certainly fewer Shermans or Irvings, fewer Jewish Sandras or Janeens.

If my general impression about the spread of renaming is right, the question Why comes up. What are the young, whatever their creed or color, fighting against? I believe they're fighting against being like us. Ignorant though they are, they are less ignorant than their parents. They know about more and better options in life. They know about new options. And in our culture the urge to reject the past generations has always been stronger than anywhere else. "I have lived some thirty years on this planet," Henry Thoreau was saying belligerently over a century ago, "and I have yet to hear the first syllable of valuable or even earnest advice from my seniors."

And yet . . . I may be wrong about the extent of renaming and wrong, further, about my hypothesis. In evidence, a bit of research a friend of mine and I did a few weeks ago about the past as a predictor of the present. The evidence comes from the commencement programs of the University of Maryland for 1970, 1960, and 1950. We scrutinized the given names of all students listed as graduating in each of those years.

The class of 1970 was named in the new era that burst upon us after the end of World War II. I searched for hints of fresh trends and novelties. I found a roll call of the obvious, a recital of the not-new. The most popular names for male graduates were, in descending order: John, Robert, William, James, Richard, David, Michael, Thomas, and Charles. The female graduates fared slightly better; occasionally their parents thought they could indulge themselves. The top name was Mary, and I knew even before looking at the lists that it was a perennial favorite. But the names that followed swung, at least a little. They were Linda, Susan, and Patricia. It was also a good year for Nancy and Diana.

Who do you think led the list for male graduates in 1960? John, Robert, William, James, Richard, and Charles. Among the female graduates, Mary of course. But it proved to be a banner year for Barbara, who stood second, and Patricia, who ranked third.

Finally, back to 1950. The male names? Now, all together, repeat with me: John, Robert, William, and so on. And the most popular female name was . . . Mary.

I suppose that—though the thought wins no prizes for novelty—we exaggerate the degree of change. With loving allowance for Henry Thoreau, we still are pretty much the creatures of the past. We follow the new style in manners, clothes, and cars; but at the primal level we cling to the old.

So I watch with appreciation when my ex-students marry and start rearing a family. Some of the farthest out among them never toilet-train their babies, so their apartments smell like a chamber pot. But most seem to raise their infants as their parents did. For example, a "good" baby is one who doesn't cry, who responds to training. And do my rebellious ex-students name their offspring Mao or Che or Eldridge C.? Rarely if ever. Instead they demonstrate a reluctant preference for John, Robert, William—and inevitably Mary, pardon me, Mari.

38

Getting Well Adjusted
with Weeds

When it comes to really heavy, thoughtful statements my favorite gardening editor, Woody Woodbin, wins the plume every time. Sometimes by thirty-one lengths. I say this because I've just finished poring over his latest column in the paper. It's about weeds.

Let me make you a sporting offer. Without reading any further, guess how Woody opens this column. What is the most solemn, banal, and commonplace observation you could imagine? Give up? I quote it word for word: "Weeds are a serious problem for farmers and gardeners."

Woody provides an embarrassment of riches, with more quotable quotes than I can ever find space for. Let me offer you one or two, however, of the real dandies. Here is Woody on what we should do about weeds: "Pull them up." He continues shrewdly: "When they are small they are easy to pull up." He adds that they sometimes appear suddenly in the garden and "gardeners wonder where they came from." I can visualize my favorite gardener—a small, stooped Yorkshireman called Wuggins, with gnarled and knowing hands—peering around and demanding loudly (in an accent I couldn't possibly imitate) where all those bloody weeds came from. Well, Wuggins, old friend, I don't know but Woody does. They came by air, by water, and by animal. And by something Woody mysteriously terms "man's devices." I presume he means the McCormick Patent Weed Proliferator or the Handy-Dandy Weed Spreader or perhaps those aerosol cans of Weed Grow.

But Woody offers us more than mystery. He offers us statistics. Most of them I beg you not to read if you're quickly discouraged, for they are chilling.

Item: more than 10,000 (10,157?) weed seeds were discovered by one sharp-eyed researcher in a patch of soil only three feet square and ten inches deep. This agronomist, named H. J. C. Clipser, sacrificed a full set of fingernails in doing his research. Item: not only are there a lot of different kinds of weeds (7,301) but many thrive on Geritol. Says Woody: "Many of the weed seeds will survive in the soil for 70 years and some for four score and ten."

After this lurch into poetry Woody closes his column and so lets me soar on with mine. For I want to use the rest of my essay to show how Woody is wrong, all wrong, and why he has lapsed into dreadful error. Since I disdain such a cheap trick as keeping you in suspense, I'll tell you the secret now and then adorn it with chapter and verse.

The secret is to redefine weeds. Call them "weeds" if they're delicate, quick to droop, hard to nurture; if they are a meal for every insect masticating in the garden. Roses, violets, azaleas, pansies, nasturtiums, dahlias—they all cry for care. So ignore them. Tomatoes, peas, lettuce, sweet corn—let them wither on the stalk or vine.

Learn instead to cherish the thistle, the burdock, the sturdy dandelion. Savor the folk poetry to be found, for instance, in cat's ear, crabgrass, crazyweed, creeping buttercup, sheep's sorrel, spotted spurge, and sandbur.

Compose a sonnet on the spotted spurge; make up a madrigal on cat's ear; paint the glowing colors of the creeping buttercup. Or the spurry. If you haven't glimpsed the spurry in full bloom, you haven't seen the sunrise of the weedy world. Ochre, azure, and maroon.

As we learn to love these newfound plants and flowers, we can begin to crossbreed them. We can join the gaudiness of one with the aroma of another. Imagine the dandelion crossed with the skunkweed. Or the bindweed with the beggar-tick.

Then we can originate new and more splendid weeds in our greenhouses and laboratories. I propose only a few, simply furnishing the name to spur you to create the actuality. For example: idiot-grass, the wottle-bait, creeping ulch, the finneran, purple teepo, and the snooge. Look into the future. Can't you see yourself at end of day gazing proudly at your weed garden? It needs practically no care, no labor. At rare intervals you may have to uproot a lily or scotch a rose. Once or twice a season you may want to wet down the bricklike Maryland clay that makes your garden, but once or twice will be enough.

And what about Woody? He'll write just as sagely about weeds as about vegetables or flowers. But he'll write with much more contentment, in a world devoid of difficulties. He'll start a column with: "Orchids are no problem to weed farmers and gardeners. They pull up easy."

39

Homage to Richard Hart

"Good God, Doc, what do those kids want?" Remember that plaint which I once quoted from my milkman as he left a quart of homogenized and a pint of half & half? I've heard it from others too, blue-collar and white-collar, male and female, middle-aged and not so middle-aged. They all think, with a certain envy, of everything today's college student has. To them today's campus is nirvana.

I can't blame them. And yet I can't blame my students either. My sympathies go out to some if not all of them, because they're in a bind. They know, morning, noon, and night, what they don't want to do in life. But they don't know what they do want to do. I won't headline this finding as a whizbang novelty—it's been announced before—but it has an unexpected poignancy when applied to bright, fresh-eyed twenty-two-year olds who find themselves immobilized.

Put yourself in their place. You don't crave an eight to five existence hinging on a lifelong commute. You don't want to peddle plastic from stoop to stoop or door to door. You don't want to be a housewife all your life, or some shill's secretary. Male or female, you don't yearn to settle down in one of the well-known houses of ticky-tacky.

On the other hand you don't want to play Henry Thoreau either. Face it: beneath your frayed blue jeans and raunchy shirts lies a liking for luxury. You relish costly music and high-quality pot. No cabin by a pond for you, with beans for breakfast, lunch, and supper.

Nor do you, if I may say so, yearn to be a passionate disciple of Fidel, Che, or Mao. The tough life of the real revolutionary would turn you off. Of the tens of thousands of our campus militants, only a handful travel to Cuba each summer to cut sugar cane fourteen hours a day. Ordered to spend half of each school year shoveling night-soil onto the collective fields at Chungking, you'd split.

So what's left, you properly and cooperatively ask? What's left, I think, is the spirit if not the substance of Thoreau's life. A life lived by an individual and drawing on that individual's deepest capacities. If that sounds to you like just another piety, let me cite a pleasant and provocative instance, the career of Richard Hart.

If you leafed through the *Sunday Sun* a few weekends ago (adv.—no charge), you saw John Dorsey's essay on him, occasioned by the fact that he's just retired after forty-three years at the Enoch Pratt Library. Two things struck me while I read. One, how much he's been his own person; the other, how varied and interesting the things he has done. For example, as a youth he joined the merchant marine instead of enrolling at Johns Hopkins, shipping on a melancholy tub christened the *Quaker City*. With him he lugged a big bag of books and a small one of clothes. The *Quaker City* broke up in a hurricane in 1929, he told John Dorsey, so he "was bunged up a bit and came home." The echoes resound of Melville and Masefield, of Conrad and Kipling.

Yet the result was, with the brisk turn toward the unexpected which has marked his career, that he didn't go to sea again but to library school. If that seems to you something of a dull thud, I can only tell you that it was the doorway to those forty-three years at the Enoch Pratt. Very good years too, though a fellow could get a bit bunged up from time to time even at the Enoch Pratt.

And years of tireless ingenuity and inventiveness, of scheming how to serve the readers best. As I took around me nowadays, it seems to me that the agents of evil own all the energy and zeal.

But I'm wrong. Richard Hart has both, and they are transparently on the side of good. And not the good which H. L. Mencken derided as snuffling Puritanism but the good which has a gleam in its eye and an engaging grin.

Further, he has been a friend of change. In the old days the literature department at Pratt was almost like a club, of writers as well as readers; the atmosphere was urbane. Today the department serves an altered public, younger on the average, far less well-read, but—at any rate—reading. The popularity of English literature among the department's readers has sunk; that of American literature has ballooned; that of Black Studies is on the rise, along with Women Studies.

He has not demanded, even of good ideas, that they remain for eternity. After all, a good idea too has its term. Here are a few instances from many in the Dorsey article. The yearly poetry contest for Black students which he and Professor Nick Aaron Ford of Morgan College ran during the late 1940s and early 1950s. The Pratt Wednesday noon talks which he organized for nearly thirty years. I spoke for him several times and won't forget the fire-breath'd ghost of Walt Whitman who rose to confound me the time I'd announced that Walt was the biggest fraud in American literature. In radio, the series entitled "Voices of Maryland." In television, the Pratt-Walters Gallery show which ran for eight years. Back at the library again, the "Afternoons with the Poets" from 1935 to 1954.

However, Richard Hart has been much more than an organizer. It's plain that individuals concern him more than agencies. A student searching sadly for a footnote reference, a man browsing for a book to take his mind off his troubles, a young woman reading toward liberation. Richard Hart has seen and helped each—as an individual.

Without question Richard Hart's life has been overburdened and will continue to be. He attracts responsibilities like a magnet. But I've known him for years and I don't worry about it anymore. He relishes being overburdened. He not only wears a crown of thorns, he presses it down a bit every now and then.

We're lucky he's that way. Baltimore is the better for Richard Hart.

40

You've Come a Long Way, Babay, but You've Still Got Further To Go

The original advertising for Virginia Slims ("Slimmer than the fat cigarettes men smoke") drew the hostile, hot-eyed attention of several women's groups because it smacked of the sex market. It featured skinny, sexy females who stressed their skinniness and sexiness as they announced proudly through their cigaret smoke, "You've come a long way, Baby." Sweating visibly at the women's criticism, the manufacturer decided to improve his image by sponsoring a winter tennis circuit for professional women players. Last week was Washington's turn to be on the circuit. I went to watch the finals.

I was charmed. I found that girls were still different from boys, that women were still different from men. This is a sexist thing to say, I know. But I decline to trundle out my credentials for Women's Liberation; for anyone who wishes to inquire they lie among the Bode archives ribboned and ready.

In the finals Margaret Court played Kerry Melville. According to the glossy booklet the promoters put out, Margaret Court comes from Perth, Australia. She stands five feet ten inches, weighs about 140 pounds, and hits the tennis ball as if she hated it. Many women players pat the ball; not Margaret. When she serves she rears to her full height, hikes her racket as high as she can reach, and then whams it down on the ball. She wears a white tennis dress to which she attaches a starchy blue collar. She is thirtyish, married, and the mother of little Danny.

Kerry Melville is five years younger and looks ten. She looks in fact like a girl. She ties back her brown hair with a ribbon; her tennis dress is pink; her underpants have rows of ruffles. She is four inches shorter and twenty pounds lighter than Margaret Court, and she gives the impression of slimness even though her thighs are full and muscular. She too comes from Australia.

Both are among the best women players in the world, with Margaret clearly ranking ahead of Kerry. They walk out into the steamy indoor arena, at Linden Hill in the Washington suburbs, to generous applause. They rally the ball back and forth casually; then the match begins. Margaret Court serves first. She's been in the players' lounge talking offhand with her husband while she holds Danny. She isn't psyched up, so she promptly loses her service in the first game. For many players this would be a disaster but not for her. She simply breaks through Kerry's serve in turn. The score stands at 1–1. Then she takes command.

Her powerful forehand streaks into corners Kerry can't reach. Her backhand slices off from the green carpeting of the indoor court. It isn't that Kerry can't return any shots. She hits back most of them and many become winners. But she doesn't hit back enough. Too many sail out or plunk against the net cord and then drop back on her side. According, again, to that glossy program, Kerry's best shots are a forehand which slides to the opponent's backhand and a delicate drop shot which dies on hitting the ground. All to no avail, as they say in the story books. She fails to win another game in the first set. At set point I hear from her a small sigh.

Nothing more, though. Like all Australian players she shows style whether she wins or loses. Old Harry Hopman, the great Australian coach, believed in building character in order to win at tennis. His players rarely glare at the linesmen, fling their rackets into the stands, or indulge in any of the rowdy theatricals that the Romanian players, for instance, savor so much.

As the match proceeds I see with satisfaction that the crowd too has style. There are no boos, no bottles tossed on the court; only applause or a long "Ah-h-h" of appreciation.

121

Play rolls on. Margaret keeps up her winning points. Her sign is Cancer, while Kerry's is Leo; and to my friends who are astrology heavies the difference in the score takes some explaining. Anyhow, they are both females, and all through the play I see an endearing feminine gesture which somehow takes the hard edge off the contest. It's the habit both players have of tugging up their shoulder straps after almost every point.

The match done, Mrs. Sargent Shriver presents Margaret with the $6,000 first prize. Danny is there too. He pulls at the microphone cord, interrupting his mother. Mrs. Shriver and the crowd laugh, and then the crowd streams out into the chilly, sunny afternoon.

Is there a moral here? I think so and I'm glad. But I admit that when Margaret played Bobby Riggs, I was for her all the way.

[*I do an occasional sports column and I wrote this one in March 1973. I preserve it here on the off chance that though the rankings in the world of women's tennis have shifted, I'm still on the track of a Profound Truth.*]

41

Happy Birthday,
Mercury's Mencken

I've always thought that on September 12 the Baltimore schools should lock doors for the day, the weather should turn bright and crisp, the stores should give away all merchandise costing less than a dollar, and the president of the Mercantile-Safe Deposit should stand benignly above Hopkins Plaza letting $2 bills drift down on the cheering spectators. And the *Sunpapers* should be printed not on their usual stock of dingy white but on cool green.

For the twelfth is St. Henry's Day, H. L. Mencken's birthday, and the green paper would memorialize the green cover of the *American Mercury*, which he shaped into the sprightliest magazine this country has had so far. You snort and call me biased? Not a bit. I grant you that the *New Yorker* still has its moments, that at times the *Saturday Evening Post* (remember?) purveyed more than apple pie, that the *Atlantic* before it became besotted by the ghetto printed some literature. But you blow the dust of thirty or forty years from their files, to go back to the time when the *Mercury* flourished, and you find them dismally dated. Not the *Mercury*.

Of course I concede that it was a creature of its era, showing the shallow-pated prejudices of the 1920s. Yet it often transcended them. In terms of that mix of the universal and particular which we look for in literature, the *Mercury* did well—especially if we remember that it wasn't written For the Ages.

The other day I was at the Library of Congress scanning the circulation figures for the *Mercury* during Mencken's editorship. They had just been opened to researchers. The best year, with the biggest sales, proved to be 1927. I happen to own a copy of the April 1927 issue and I'd like to share it with you. It is, I think, a nice combination of Then and Now.

The inside cover carries an ad on automobile safety headed "The National Safety Council Says So!" What it says is that the safest car is the Stutz. Think of that, boys and girls. Today the Ford Company grows fat, the General Motors cars rip up the road, and the Chrysler group still shoves speed at you. But when did you last see a Stutz? Interestingly, Chrysler also took an ad in the April 1927 issue, and on its list of allurements it put speed and "dash" first and safety last.

The striking thing about the rest of the advertising is how much comes from book publishers. Though the House of Knopf naturally ranks first since it published the magazine, there are a dozen pages from rival firms. Most of what they herald is as forgotten as the Stutz, but by no means everything. Not books by Edwin Arlington Robinson, W. B. Yeats, Hemingway, or Sinclair Lewis. Considering what it has done to book-buying, television has much to answer for.

The lead article is an exposé of a still highly effective and at the same time dignified monopoly, the Associated Press. It's followed by "Go Down, Death!", one of the Black poet James Weldon Johnson's finest poems. It catches a Black idiom in its lines without literally transcribing it; it's an impressive, haunting lyric. Among the half dozen short articles—all brisk, all bearing the marks of Mencken's sharp editorial pen—we see one on "The Youngest Generation" as always, and another on the great Pooh-Bah of the American steel industry, Judge Elbridge Gary. That one is worth noting for the lovely pomposity of the quotes from him. For instance, when United States Steel was forced by law to cut its work day from twelve to eight hours, the judge announced on high, "Our men will be sadly disappointed at the change. . . . We can only hope they will take it good-naturedly."

Still another investigates how much it costs us to bury a congressman or a senator. The answer, with examples, is "Plenty." Even in 1927 it cost the taxpayer $11,000 to send four senators to their permanent rest.

One article stirred up some hornets. "Portrait of a Rolling-Mill" pictured the griminess of mass education at New York University. Evidently written from inside, it was signed by one Malcolm B. Susser. However, though they searched vengefully through their faculty rosters, the angry deans at NYU never found his name and never discovered who he really was. Today my spies tell me that he was a professor of English—a member of a tricky tribe if I ever saw one.

The literary pieces, aside from a sardonic playlet by my neighbor James M. Cain, didn't bowl me over, I confess. But the essays and reviews by Mencken and his partner George Jean Nathan sparkled. They appeared in the so-called Departments of the magazine. Nathan did "The Theatre" with a verve which helped to make him the most readable drama critic of the period. Mencken did the witty editorials (imagine: witty editorials!) and the book reviews in "The Library." His lead review was of Sinclair Lewis's new novel, *Elmer Gantry*, which caricatured revivalists and revivalism. He hailed it as better than *Main Street* or *Babbitt*. I read Mencken's opening paragraphs with an incredulous eye—old *Gantry* couldn't be that good—but then something happened. I could see how he became a notable critic, and not simply a slasher, because he communicated more than a pinch of his enthusiasm to me. Though I didn't feel he could be right about this brash antitheological tract, I promised myself that I'd take a fresh look at it.

The general magazine, as of this afternoon, lies dying. *Harpers* suffers pitiably. The *Atlantic* has left literature for hoked-up social science. The *New Yorker* suffers from an identity crisis that sends it orbiting between the *Nation* and *Punch*. And I find nothing to take the general magazine's place. The new trend, I'm assured, is toward the very special journal. But the *Meat Renderers' Monthly* or *Mortuary Notes* somehow don't substitute for the *Mercury* and its collateral descendants.

42

Pornography at Maryland: Trials and Triumphs

Who cries that American ingenuity and perseverance are dead? Who bleats that Young America can't cope with crises? Or that the college student can do little but laze on his back, counting his toes or popping Pronto pills.

Look at the students who run the *Argus*, the campus magazine at the University of Maryland. For them next week will mark a victory for dogged endeavor. The pornography number, the one with the prize winners in the *Argus*'s national pornography contest, is finally coming out. The way it's been done has been to imbed the whole 52-page issue in a 120-page special "non-pornography" number. The ham in the sandwich.

It's taken since last fall to achieve this triumph, and the tale is an inspirational one. Let me tell it and also share my own reading of the prize-winning articles with the many of you who won't be able to see the issue.

I'd better begin when, disguised as Humphrey Bogart, I interviewed Al Isaacs. He's the student editor of the magazine, a mustachioed senior, very bright, and a master of the put-on. He received me affably in the *Argus* office, treating me in fact almost as an equal, while the strobe lights flashed and Adolf and His Anteaters boomed out their zoomy music.

Al's contest had gained national attention, much of it apoplectic, when the *Argus* announced last fall, with a sidelong grin, that it would hold the tourney and print the three winners. Any kind of pornography that could be written was eligible. Vice-President Agnew immediately demanded, on the Paul Talley Talk Show, that everyone involved be broken on the wheel. Two members of the Maryland Assembly sponsored a bill dissolving the university and replacing it with a chicken-rendering institute. Several state senators wrote the *Argus* office, in pencil, demanding that copies of the contest number be mailed to them in plain wrappers the instant it appeared.

The senators are still waiting. I'm not, however. While talking earnestly with Al, I was able to smuggle a typescript copy into a seat pocket of my pleated pants. True, it meant that after our interview I had to back out, a little like retreating before royalty —bowing, scraping, and never turning around. But I imagine that Al attributed my odd exit to my respect for Student Power.

I had only a dim idea of the *Argus*'s trouble till he told me in the course of the interview. He confessed that he enjoyed setting the campus administration on its ear. Chancellors and deans were easy to discumbobulate (my word; Al used an obscenity), and he could dodge any dead cats from their direction. They could hardly stop the contest. What hurt, however, was a flank attack, bitter and unexpected, from the university's cell of Woman's Liberation. Frostily its leaders charged the *Argus* with using women as sex objects. Looking gimlet-eyed at Al, they put their position. Women's Liberation had no right to tell him to kill the pornography number. That would interfere with freedom of the press. But they wanted him to understand that anyone who published the winning entries automatically qualified as a Male, Motherhugging, Fascist Pig.

The *Argus,* backpedaling like a boxer after being decked, announced to everyone in earshot that what it really yearned to do was to encourage literary quality and that pornography was merely a vehicle. Excellence alone was what the *Argus* was after. No offense intended.

When that hassle finished and Women's Liberation was partly appeased, the editorial staff winnowed through the pile of entries, looking, it must be reported, a bit apprehensively over its collective shoulder. Finally it finished separating the pornographic wheat from the chaff. It pasted up the winners and completed the layout for the issue. Then it mailed it to the printers, the Hyattsville firm of Erdelman & Herdelman. Unknown to the *Argus*, not one of the firm's typesetters fails to have an American flag decal on his car window, along with two bumper stickers, one saying "America, Love It or Leave It" and the other "Hyattsville, the Navel of the Universe."

The high-minded typesetters scanned the entries, turned beet-red under their paper hats, and declared that By God they wouldn't set this mucked up stuff. What would the Missis say if she ever found out?

It wasn't easy to dig up another printer. But they did finally, smothering his pangs of conscience with money. The 120-page special issue cost the *Argus* a mint, which is why there won't be many copies to sell next week. However, I have my trusty typescript right here. I'm ready to score a beat and give you the essence of each winning entry—and to quote its most erotic passage as well.

First place went to a short story "Rutabaga," in which a mother falls in love with her vegetable son. The climactic sentence: "Beet, me, baby, beet me!"

Second place went to the sexual fantasy of an electronic computer. It was titled "It must be Jelly 'Cause Jam don't Shake like That." The peak passage: "ISLE OF VIEW. ISLE OF VIEW. ISLE OF VIEW."

And third place went to "Making It in Mexico," the story of an aging couple's subtropical passion. The punch line: "Owooo!"

Sort of makes you proud to be an American, doesn't it?

[*The events I embalm here took place during the academic year 1970–71. The column appeared in June 1971.*]

43

Bards on Battle Bent

Maryland poets are on the march. From Rising Sun and Silver Spring, from Frederick and Frostburg, from Greater Baltimore and Lesser Baltimore, they are advancing on Annapolis.

Two highly placed but prosaic Democratic legislators have just introduced a bill to strip the Honorable Vincent Burns of his permanent title of Maryland's poet laureate. The venerable Vincent is fighting back with all the vim of his eighty-eight years. Most young Maryland poets have known no other laureate. He was appointed by Governor Millard Tawes during a golden reign when the state had no problems that couldn't be postponed. The governor himself was, and is, a poetry buff whose repertory of Longfellow lyrics is longer than his arm. You should hear him recite, from memory, "The Skeleton in Armor." When the governor's voice breaks at "She was a Prince's child/I but a Viking wild," it's a rare cheek that isn't tear-stained.

Burns himself during his long tenure has received many honors. He has been president of the Grand Union of Sentient Hymnologists (GUSH). He has been awarded the Order of Merit (Fourth Class) by the Albanian government. Maryland Kiwanians have named him The Poet We'd Like to have Meet the Wife.

There is no doubt that he has built an impressive following. The

129

octogenarian bard is much more prolific and popular than his carping younger colleagues. He is a popular poet in the grandest sense. For him, rhyming "June" and "moon" is a wild adventure. He loves iambic pentameter and only after severe thought will he tiptoe into trochees. He eschews (that's a word I don't get to use every day) four-letter words unless they're scrubbed squeaky clean. He celebrates the acknowledged great men and great occasions of Maryland.

His hymns to Governor Tawes were rousing ones and found their way into many a Marylander's heart. He pleased Governor Agnew for all time by writing an "Ode to the Agnew Dog." Burns sensed that Spiro Agnew was the sort of man whose favorite poem would be a poem about a dog, so the ode is rich and full. In fact, it devotes four fat stanzas to "Zorba's" four brindled paws.

Gossip at the state house says that Burns came a cropper, however, when Governor Mandel took office. My Annapolis spies say that some sonneteer misled the poet laureate about how to pronounce the new governor's name. Consequently, when Burns rose on inauguration day to celebrate the governor before the host of assembled dignitaries he chanted, turning to him, "Governor Mandel, Governor Mandel / No one's fit to latch your sandal." Though the governor started and then smiled, it was seen that he spoke a few words to his equerry, who took notes.

At any rate, the move is now under way to dethrone Vincent Burns. The move has collected—as the threatened laureate sees it—a motley array of supporters. Their Popular Front is the Maryland Poetry Society, a statewide organization of dissidents. Most members, according to the venerable Vincent, are callow, radical, and allergic to rhyme. The laureate's followers have mounted a counter-campaign in which they point out that Communist poetry likewise eschews rhyme and that its rhythms, furthermore, sound highly irregular.

Plans were announced yesterday by the anti-Burns faction for a Poetry-In at the state capitol. They intend to bombard the Assembly with ballads, and indeed ballades. They intend to lay their bodies on the line, so that the legislators will have to step on prone poets to enter. Then the dissidents intend to have pictures taken of their ordeal, to use in the next election. They will publish the photos with captions like "This is what Delegate Plimsoll thinks of culture" or "State Senator Saltt stepping on the inheritors of Shakespeare." They predict that many a legislator will never return to Annapolis, except as a tourist bringing his Uncle Wilberforce and Aunt Wilma from Toledo to see the Naval Academy.

Where do I stand, as a part-time poet? Let me tell you plainly where I stand . . . What other state has a poet laureate like Vincent Burns? What other state, for that matter, has a poet laureate? (I merely pose the rhetorical question.) Let me call the roll of his most moving poems: "Sunset over Silver Spring," "Barbara Fritchie, Mother of Mine," "Louis Goldstein, You're Never Gilt to Me," "In Westminster the Waters are Wailing" (thirty-seven stanzas, each with refrain), and "Maryland, My Maryland" (no more blood and gore; the laureate has sanitized every stanza).

Fellow bards, on to Annapolis! There hasn't been such excitement since two philosophers at Vassar had a fist fight over metaphysics.

131

44

The Big Steal

Can you stand a five-minute homily? My message, as a jackleg historian, is that many things have been stolen from the American people. Sometimes with their connivance, often without their opposition. Forests, parks, houses, money. And the air. It was taken from us, first in small pieces and then in enormous chunks. Now it's being sold back to us, or rather, rented.

I'm thinking about television of course. If you've lived in Britain you know how good the BBC is, and how even commercial television rises far above the American level in order to meet the BBC's competition.

The terrifying thing is that we've now raised a generation who've never seen what television can really be. They haven't the dimmest notion of what they've missed; for them the salad days of television never existed.

But some of you remember them. It wasn't Culture they offered us; it was largely entertainment—but good entertainment and not interrupted every ten minutes.

We watched Uncle Miltie faithfully, and if we didn't have a set ourselves, we walked over to our more enterprising neighbors. They not only let us stare at the little screen but even fed us chip-dip and popcorn. Then we bought our own sets and discovered there was more than Uncle Miltie. We—or anyway

I—discovered a program purportedly for children, "Kukla, Fran, and Ollie." It was a puppet show created by a genius, Burr Tillstrom, and featuring a gracious lady, Fran Allison. I discovered a show called "Stud's Place," set in a Chicago bar where the characters actually ad-libbed their lines. It had the freshness, spontaneity, and sometimes the pleasant awkwardness of the Italian *commedia del' arte*. And then came "Garroway at Large." Few who saw it, late on Sunday nights, failed to feel its glow. For grace, elegance, and wit, no other show could surpass it. Yet many of the other shows had some freshness too, as well as the surprises that go with being unrehearsed on a new medium. I shall never forget the time that the Ritz Brothers ended ten minutes early and the desperate humor of their attempts to fill the yawning gap.

This was the period when the brightest talent was to be found in Chicago; and the Chicago period was an almost pastoral one. But then the big advertisers and their hard-nosed agents decided that the medium was for them. The shows were gradually shifted to New York and near Madison Avenue. The shows became slicker, the commercials longer. The turning point came in the early 1950s. "Kukla, Fran, and Ollie," having shrunk from a daily half-hour to five minutes, now wistfully disappeared. "Garroway at Large" was shifted from the late Sunday evenings to early prime time, became hard and glittering—and failed. But there were still good shows and some of the best of television drama that we were ever to see. Gradually, however, the New York period drew to a close and television found in Hollywood its new center of gravity.

But before it left New York, television provided culture as well as entertainment. The most eminent example was the Sunday afternoon "Omnibus" program, underwritten by the Ford Foundation. For a few years the American public, with Alistair Cooke's guidance, had windows opened up on the world of the fine arts which have been shut ever since.

And then television moved to Hollywood; and in Hollywood it has stayed, with its cheap, trivial, and often nasty twenty-minute movies. Yet even Hollywood's limitations can be transcended sometimes, and there've been occasional good shows coming from the converted movie lots and sound stages. The trouble is that the industry has showed a growing tendency to eat its young. After a while it has usually devoured even its liveliest shows—even the lucrative comedies. Only "Lucy," without Desi, has survived. From the "Sergeant Bilko" series to the delightful "Hennessy" show, all the others have been dropped.

The creative talents were so steadily frustrated that most of them are now gone. Only here and there do we see a survivor who has decided dourly to give the advertisers what they want.

My feeling is that the programs will seem steadily more outlandish, more quirky. The commercials will increase gradually but relentlessly until we spend more time watching advertising than anything else. This has been the history of television so far; I see no reason for feeling that it will not continue. And then what will the hapless public do? I predict that it will learn to like the commercials, and will sit idly watching them. You and I will be there too. We'll still squirm on viewing some unctuous idiot as he assures us that it is all right for us to sweat, as long as we plaster ourselves with Ono, or some smily pitchman who promises us all the sex we want if we buy the right car. But we'll watch anyway—and we'll relish the good commercials. I know: I see it starting now in myself. I like that Eastern Airlines ad with all those bird-types looking startled in it. I like the "Taste of Kent" with its perfect musical and visual timing. I like the "Xerox" ads because of the highbrow pitch they make.

We might as well, I suppose, make the best of it. If, ending as I began, we take the long view and start back in the late 1940s, we will see a steady deterioration. It is punctuated by assurances from the broadcasters that they want to serve us, from the regulatory agencies that they'll guard the public interest, and from Congress that no federal bureaucrat is going to interfere with our freedom on the airwaves. The net result is that the decline has continued. I don't see that we can do a thing about it. We might as well adjust to it and settle back.

What I do at the commercials is to watch the background instead of listening to the shouting for the product. By now I've looked at enough backgrounds so that I can get a sense of the America advertisers think will appeal to us most. It's also the

America, in part at least, which they've filched from us. Trees, open spaces, meadows, privacy, sunsets, smalltown porches, wide lawns, picnics, neighborhood parties, friendship, trust, and security. Naturally they never show ghettos, shoddy beehive housing, dark streets with crime threatening. But they help to create it all.

45

How I Got Charisma
—And You Can Too

Last Christmas? Last Christmas I was an ungrateful lout. As you may recall, perhaps too clearly, I said hard words about the plumage my family bought me. I didn't like being gauded up, thank you, I told them. The plumage went back to the store and I spent all last year in my oxford-gray suit with the inch-wide lapels, my black shoes over white socks, and my pencil-thin blue tie. The only time people noticed me was when I stepped on their foot.

But not now. No longer. And it's all because of this Christmas. My family fortunately remembered Thomas Jefferson's splendid dictum, "It takes time to persuade people to do even what is for their own good." Once again on Christmas morning I found myself opening packages wildly colored and weirdly wrapped. They came from such mid-town shops as Toast & Strawberries, Generation Gapp, and Kazoo.

While my family watched nervously I eviscerated box after box. As it turned out, the most striking present was a pair of elephant-leg, plum-colored levis. Close behind the levis in pizzaz came the matching coat. Except for its flaring lapels it was cut like an Eisenhower jacket of World War II. (Dad, explain that to the kids and tell them it was named after Ike, not Milton.) I found myself the lucky winner of not one but two body shirts, one a yellow V-neck and the other a puce round-neck, both guaranteed to cling like a second skin. I also received a variety of oddments. First among them I rank my new bow tie. I'll tell you what it's like but it takes an effort to visualize it. It's a tie-dyed McGregor plaid. Though it doesn't light up or flash on and off, it really doesn't need to.

But the charisma, you demand greedily, what about the charisma? Well, I'll tell you. Deciding that when you can't beat them you might as well join them, I struggled into my Christmas clothes on Christmas day—and I haven't shucked them since! Where I was ignored before, I'm now the object of fascinated attention. Persons of all ages and sexes look at me with interest. In fact several times when I've chanced to turn around, I've seen them staring at my back. More than one of them has smiled invitingly, or even leered. Because the weather has been frosty I've added a knee-length wool scarf, of the sort that Alec Guinness wore in, I believe, *The Lavender Hill Mob*.

Naturally I'm thinking of going into politics, or at least becoming a social lion. I haven't decided just where to pitch my political tent, in Roland Park or Ruxton, in Hawkins Point or Highlandstown. But I anticipate that wherever I go I'll find lively, interested audiences. They won't have to be unanimously favorable. I've already discovered that all you need in politics is attention.

Attention . . . and perhaps a platform. Mine is ready. So is my slogan, which sums up the platform. "Charisma for All." I admit confidentially that I'll focus on the educated but insecure voter. Look at me, I'll say. See what these brave Christmas clothes have done for me. I was a ninety-seven-pound weakling; bullies could kick sand in my face. Now, in my plummy Eisenhower jacket and elephant levis I stand six feet tall and four feet broad. Nobody messes with me. Clothes, the right clothes, make the man and woman both.Thomas Carlyle had the same idea, and his book *Sartor Resartus* was a bestseller in its time. He offered instructions on how the tailor should retailor, and all Britain listened. We should take a leaf from his book, maybe a whole chapter.

Dress with daring. Let it all hang out, as the kids used to put it. With those new clothes will come a new confidence, I promise you. "Charisma," you'll be able to say, "you belong to me!"

46

Capitol Campus—Coming

As colleges go, Washington's Federal City College is still very new and very Black. Its birth pangs have been prolonged and painful. Student riots, faculty protests, and administrative chicanery have marred its early years. Because Washington has become so largely Black, some factions at the college have fought to make it not a liberal-arts institution but a staging ground for Black enterprises. At one point there was the effort to introduce "Black mathematics" into the mathematics curriculum. And to introduce "techniques of the African hunt" into the physical education courses.

Nothwithstanding, I predict a handsome future for the college. I'm confident that it will grow into an eminent institution able to satisfy both the demands of the Black community and the needs of a national university.

The problem has been, I think, that few people recognize the magnitude of the difficulties and the fact that they've existed ever since the District of Columbia was a town of mud roads and magnificent—but empty—distances. Each of the other great capitals of the world, from Moscow to Tokyo, is the seat of a great national university. But not Washington.

It seems to me that this is a grave fault and that the blame lies clearly in the profound indifference, over the past century and a half, of two groups: the members of Congress and the leaders of Washington's white community. Almost from the outset the ingredients for a national university were at hand. All it required was the will to assemble them. On taking a look at the history of higher education in Washington, I find that time after time farsighted individuals proposed plans or led movements for such a university. Time after time they announced eagerly that the right moment had arrived. And time after time the Congress turned its back on them, and the white community let the plans wither without a qualm.

As far back as 1806, during Thomas Jefferson's first term as president, the first notable proposal for a great university was laid before Congress and the people. They ignored it as they ignored its successors. But for those of us who value education the proposal has a certain melancholy interest, and so I give its highlights.

The idea emerged from the lively mind of Joel Barlow. He was an author who still retains at least a corner in our anthologies of American literature. Also, he was a widely traveled diplomat in those days of the young republic, who had a chance to visit European universities. He submitted his idea in the shape of a printed *Prospectus of a National Institution.* Many of his suggestions still seem sensible. He saw the chief jobs of a federal university as teaching and research (he even used the word *research*). The curriculum would include moral, political, and scientific studies —fit subjects for the new nation. It would include some study of the fine arts, which Barlow defended against the Puritan charge that they led to degeneracy.

To manage the university there would be a board of fifteen trustees and a chancellor, all appointed by the president of the United States. Attached to the university would be a university press. There would be laboratories, libraries, and gardens for botanical and agricultural experiments. The two service academies, today still at West Point and Annapolis, might also be attached; as well might a museum.

Even now Barlow's prospect can kindle enthusiasm, I think. Imagine a splendid, colonnaded campus, with much of the scientific research done today by the federal government brought together in its precincts. Imagine the National Institutes of Health and the Goddard Space Flight Center in the same spacious complex. Imagine the Library of Congress, the Smithsonian Institution, and the National Gallery all on the same stately quadrangle. And all these related by the common aim of illuminating and indeed ennobling the American mind. Imagine West Point and the Naval Academy humanized through being in a center for liberal studies. And imagine the education as not only massive but as often private and particular—a student sitting after class with a teacher.

The money for all this? The money for the federal university, Barlow believed, would come from private citizens and from the government. It would surely be provided because the need was so plain. As he said, the people are our masters; "They must be instructed in their work." He felt certain that the time was ripe. "The project," he announced, "is brought forward at a happy moment." I repeat, that was in 1806. Jefferson himself once observed—remember?—that it took time to persuade the people to do even what was for their own good. But so much time?

Anyhow, today I believe the people are at least partly persuaded. I look forward to the flourishing of the Federal City College. And in one of its halls or commons, carrels or conversation pits, I propose putting at least a small plaque to Joel Barlow.

47

Making It Easy with
Old Jules

Jules Verne, the great-grandaddy of science fiction! How I used to devour his novels in the seventh grade! My friends preferred *20,000 Leagues under the Sea* but I read and reread *The Mysterious Island*. It had less science—which I couldn't fathom anyway—and more fiction. And the fiction was the gripping Robinson Crusoe kind.

It happens that in recent years I've been spending half of each summer on an island myself. Pie-shaped and pine-covered, it lies in an outreach of Georgian Bay. Running out of reading matter there last week, including the backs of Shredded Wheat boxes, I unearthed *The Mysterious Island*. I fell on it with a glad cry, so to speak, hoping that it would refurbish the illusions of my lost youth.

I must report the result sadly. It didn't. By the time I finished the book I was firmly convinced that Jules Verne was one of the gaudiest fakers in all science fiction. In *The Mysterious Island* I found that he fobbed off on me not one but two forms of major fakery. On the Star Trek side, esoteric scientific stuff, he simply copped out. For example, when it came to explaining how the marvelous submarine *Nautilus* operated, he merely remarked that it was "by methods that will be known some day." Even for a scientific simpleton like me that was far from good enough.

On more mundane things, he rigged his story and pushed coincidence till it whimpered. His island turned out to have every natural resource you could think of. His castaways on it had every ability required to take advantage of these resources. Given a little time they could have manufactured anything but a color TV set. The telegraph, for instance, presented no problem. And after its reinvention the castaways, without once breathing hard, "put up a line of poles, equipped with glass insulators, along the road to the corral, and strung the wire between them."

There were five of these castaways, all repellently ingenious Americans, among them the engineer Cyrus Smith, the sailor Pencroff, and the boy-wonder naturalist Herbert Brown.

On my island, when it comes down to it, I couldn't even build a fire without civilization's help. On my island I couldn't even concoct a cup of tea. So I watched with irritated astonishment while Jules Verne's castaways performed their feats.

Were they short of food? Herbert and Pencroff sallied out and Herbert promptly spied some rocks adorned with shellfish. "They're mussels," Pencroff exclaimed. Not at all, pronounced Herbert looking at them with his analytic eye. "They're litho-dumuses." "Well, then," said Pencroff eagerly, "let's eat some lithodumuses." And they did; in fact they feasted. I could starve with flocks of lithodumuses around me. I wouldn't know one if it bit me in the ankle.

Did they need a sealskin bellows for their handy-dandy steel mill? A short stroll away, they found a herd of seals conveniently assembled for them. Killing a few of these huge beasts was easy. Pencroff waited till they lay napping in the sun, then sneaked up and slew them by—I quote—"hitting them on the nostrils." I'm afraid I couldn't, and wouldn't, even bang a chipmunk on the nostrils.

I just confessed that I couldn't even concoct a cup of tea. But when the castaways needed to blast through granite so that they could have an impregnable cave to live in, Cyrus Smith went off for a brief while to do some home chemistry. Soon he came striding back with a jar in his hands and announced casually about the concoction in it, "This is nitroglycerin."

Did they fancy a dinner of grouse? Pencroff made a fishing line by tying thin vines together, with a sharp curved thorn at the end for a hook. He laid the line on the ground and shortly caught three fine birds. During my next walk over the length of my island, I watched earnestly for thin vines. I pulled up the most likely and tied them together. Laying them on the ground I gave a tiny tug. The line parted in three places.

For Pencroff getting the bait was as simple as making the line. His eye fell on some "big red worms . . . crawling on the ground." Though Jules Verne never said so, I'll bet those worms were crawling toward Pencroff, not away, and with thoughts of suicide in their little hearts. No doubt they slid seraphically onto Pencroff's hook.

Any time you're cast away on my island, you'll be more than welcome. But you'd better bring along silverware for two and a dish to pass.

48

Sonnet to a Small Agency

NEA, I love you. I bless your busy, unbureaucratic heart. With such a heavy title as the National Endowment for the Arts, I'd expect to see in your cubicles or corridors flow charts; stacks of memos in sextuplicate, each with its own cold color; photos of the president adorned with laurel leaves; and throngs of functionaries in their dark suits or dun dresses, crowding the water coolers. Instead you swing, as do your jazzed-up offices.

What you've done for the arts in the few years of your existence is so salutary that I yearn to protect you. I yearn to shelter you from the cornfed congressman whose culture consists of watching reruns of reruns of "Bonanza" while guzzling Pabst Blue Ribbon. I yearn to shelter you from the blinkered liberal on Capitol Hill who says at budget time that it's going to be either bread or music. And says that our country can't afford the fine arts and social services too—this though your total budget wouldn't build even one large housing development.

I'm the more protective because I have history on my side. I can remember an episode of remarkable achievement which came to a tragicomic end.

Once before, in an era of dire necessity, we created agencies for the arts. One in particular sticks in my mind, and it can represent the others. It was the Federal Theater, founded during the Depression to give a living to theatrical workers of all sorts, from stars to stagehands. It accomplished more in four years of bad times than had been done in a generation of good ones. The total cost to the taxpayer during the life of that agency was $46 million—the cost of a single battleship in those simple days. For that amount the American public got more theater, more varied theater, and better theater than ever before.

I spare you statistics because nobody reads them. But the very range of productions the Federal Theater organized and gave is impressive: classical drama, including Christopher Marlowe's *Dr. Faustus*; modern drama, including the plays of such newcomers as Arthur Miller and Clifford Odets; dance drama; drama for children; foreign-language drama, including plays in Yiddish; musicals, including *Sing for Your Supper*; Black (or Negro then of course) drama by Black companies, including that thumping Black success *The Swing Mikado*, which made Gilbert and Sullivan shake as they never shook before; pageants, including *The Lost Colony*; and even puppet shows. There was live theater in 31 states and it was watched by 30 million persons.

In the face of this enormous achievement the Federal Theater was killed by Congress during the long, hot summer of 1939. The charges were that it harbored Communists and presented dirty plays.

The House Un-American Activities Committee, under Congressman Martin Dies, and the House Appropriations Committee led the onslaught. One highlight was provided by Congressman Joe Starnes, who demanded to know if this Christopher Marlowe fellow was a Communist. But the most memorable event was the reading aloud by Congressman Everett Dirksen, in his goose-grease voice, of the titles of some of the plays which had been given. The *Congressional Record* attests that the assembled House listened with laughter and applause.

Let me offer a few instances of what brought the House down.

"MR. DIRKSEN: There is *Up in Mabel's Room*. There is an intriguing title for you. . . . Here is another, *Be Sure Your Sex Will Find You Out* [Laughter]. Then the State Department might take note of this, *A Boudoir Diplomat*. Then there is *Around the Corner*. That must be the elusive prosperity we have been seeking for some six or seven years. . . . Next we have *Companionate Maggie,* and then this great rhetorical and intriguing question, *Did Adam Sin*? . . ."

Changing tempo and pitch, the Congressman then addressed his convulsed colleagues with the voice of reason: "Now if you want that kind of salacious tripe, very well, vote for it, but if anybody has an interest in decency on the stage, if anyone has an interest in real cultural value, you will not find it in this kind of junk."

It was in vain that Congressman Casey, from the other side of the House, rebutted stiffly that the Dirksen humor was ribald. It was in vain that the heads of the Federal Theater pointed out that these frothy comedies represented merely the smallest fraction of its varied offerings. The House voted to destroy the Theater and hooted as it did so.

That was over thirty years ago. Now the National Endowment for the Arts has made a handsome new start. Though its budget grows, it remains slender when compared with that of nearly every other agency. Yet its achievements have already been amazing in helping all the arts.

In trying to help the American theater the NEA faced a situation nearly as thorny as that of years ago. It found that dramatic productions had become so wickedly expensive that no one, except a plump businessman on a plump expense account, could afford to see them. And all that the businessman itched for was *Up in Mabel's Room* anyway. The steep expenses of Broadway productions had forced the appearance of Off-Broadway ones. The rising expenses of Off-Broadway had spawned Off-Off-Broadway. The theater once again ailed badly. Then, Enter the NEA, smiling with encouragement and brandishing not a big fistful of money but at least a small handful.

Its main aim in the last few years has been to help in the diversifying and extending of the drama, to help in increasing American creativity. In carrying out that aim it has every now and then made a blunder resounding enough to stir the shade of Everett Dirksen. But that's been the price of enterprise and shouldn't, I suggest, be begrudged.

NEA grants customarily require matching money from the

locality to which the grants are given, thereby doubling the resources for the drama. Once again, I decline to drown you in statistics on what or who has been helped, so here instead is a short selection from fiscal 1973.

To a professional theater for a six to eight state tour: Baltimore's Center Stage, $53,000.

To professional companies: Seattle's Contemporary Theater, $7,500; Abingdon, Virginia's Barter Theater, $7,500; Washington's Black Repertory Company, $50,000; and New York's LaMama Experimental Theater, $90,000.

To experimental theaters and playwright-development programs: New Orlean's Free Southern Theater, $25,000; Oklahoma City's Contemporary Arts Foundation, $3,000; and New York's defiantly named Ridiculous Theatrical Company, $10,000.

To professional theaters for young audiences, chiefly of children: Washington's Living Stage, $30,000; and New York's Paper Bag Players, $35,000.

To an organization which will subcontract its grant: New York's Theater Development Fund, $60,000.

So there we are. I've never qualified as a professional optimist, yet I concede that conditions seem better for the NEA. Everett Dirksen's son-in-law is Senator Howard Baker, and he's voted consistently to support it. I trust that's a straw in that proverbial wind.

49

American Literature
with Communist Sauce

At an embassy party in London several years ago I met the
Russian cultural attaché. He spoke almost perfect American
though he assured me that he'd never visited my country. I
promptly had a vision of that little Nebraska town in Siberia,
with its soda fountain, filling station, and ten-cent store, where
everyone was a Soviet agent learning to speak and think in
American. I felt the same way last summer when I discovered
that East Germany, most tightly controlled of the Communist
countries, was studying American literature considerably beyond
most of the western European nations.

Why was East Germany doing this? I asked myself. I wondered
if a content analysis of our current fiction was being fed into
computers to determine our psychic weaknesses. Were they min-
ing Vonnegut and James Baldwin, Bellow and Mailer, Jackie
Susann and Frank Yerby? Were they scrutinizing our poets with
the maxim in mind, Know your enemy? Or were the bureaucrats
of East Berlin dazzled by the feverish vitality of our literature?
Did they savor it as we might the prose and poetry from Saturn?

My questions were only half-facetious. I think I found at least
part of the answer to them last spring when I visited East Germany. I went on the invitation of three East German professors
whom I'd met in Washington through Communist acquaintances.

The part of the answer I'm talking about turned out to be the three professors. Emerson was right when he wrote that an institution is the lengthened shadow of a man. These men were the major Americanists in their country. Each held a chair in a leading university, one at the Friedrich Schiller University in Jena, another at the Karl Marx University in Leipzig, and the third at the Humboldt University in East Berlin. Through their enterprise and courage—it took courage especially at the start—American literature had won a place in East German higher education.

They knew when they invited me that I was no sympathizer but a standard-brand liberal Democrat. But, bless their hearts, they'd read and liked some of my books on American literature and culture, so they smoothed the way. From the time I touched down in East Berlin, I encountered consistent courtesy and considerable understanding. They said nothing about Vietnam or Israel; I ignored the marks of fresh Russian tank-treads on more than one of the streets. When we got to talking personalia I found out how two of my three hosts had acquired their interest in American life in general and American literature in particular. You wouldn't guess. They had been POWs in an American camp in Colorado during World War II.

The man I came to know best was Professor Eberhard Brüning, tall, brown-haired. He is the author of the solidest piece of scholarship so far, a study of the American theater of the 1930s, as well as of the standard handbook on American literature. I think that the handbook, *Amerikanische Literatur*, is of special interest because it illuminates the way a cosmopolitan communism views our literature.

The handbook is by no means crude. It shuns the grim idiocies which marked, for instance, our Mike Gold's or Granville Hicks's reviews of books during the Depression. It is the work of a seasoned scholar convinced that the prime purpose of literature is social but that you can't ask of all writing that it promote the class struggle.

Professor Brüning's treatment of standard American authors is objective and sensible. Confronted by Edith Wharton or Henry James, he refuses to bristle; he describes their work dispassion-

149

ately, aristocrats though they were. He deals with the American rebels such as Thoreau or Mark Twain on their own terms instead of castigating them for not being proto-Marxists.

It's in the additions to his handbook that he shows the influence of the ideology he favors. Here is the place where his American literature grows odd to American eyes. He soberly presents certain authors who have, as he sees it, advanced the workers' struggle in the United States and allots them a good many pages. They are authors almost unheard of in this country. I mentioned this fact to a young colleague of Professor Brüning. He announced that it was because they were victims of a conspiracy of silence and that all our journals had agreed to ignore them.

If so, I now propose to dent this conspiratorial silence and name at least a few. I begin with Philip Bonosky, ex-steel puddler from Pennsylvania, who has forwarded the class struggle through such a novel as *The Magic Fern*, which reveals the blighting effect of automation on the worker in American industry. Then there is Alexander Saxton, once a railroader. His novel *The Great Midland* portrays labor and life under our vicious railroad system. His *Bright Web in the Darkness* has for its theme the better life for the laborer. And there is Mitchell A. Wilson, once a doctor. His primal theme, developed in *My Brother, My Enemy* and *Meeting at a Far Meridian*, is the role of the scholar in overthrowing a capitalist society. So says the handbook.

But I don't want to stress the extreme in the East German approach to our literature. It is a broad-ranging effort. Each of the chief universities offers some courses in the subject. There is a scholarly journal on both British and American writing. There is a spate of American novels in translation, especially contemporary ones, and a trickle of novels in the original American.

All this attention seems to me largely good. Both sides benefit, I believe. After all the house of literature has many mansions, to echo a non-Marxist classic.

50

The Bathtub Renaissance

The bathtub is coming back. I make this prediction confidently though I concede that the signs are slight. Long gone are the days when C. B. De Mille based his gaudy films on the bathtub, with Gloria Swanson or Claudette Colbert lifting a dimpled knee above the foam while the audience leaned forward to gawk at whatever surfaced next. Nowadays we see only the shower bath, with its discouraging spray and opaque glass door. How can we fantasize about a shower stall?

In today's movies the anti-heroines and anti-heroes don't even wash their hands before supper. In fact they never wash anything. Even frontal nudity, that new favorite of the films, is both grimy and grim. Whether the film is Underground or Above, nobody slips gently into a warm tub. Andy Warhol's scruffy superstars— to reach back for a classic example—wouldn't have been caught dead with a bar of Ivory in their clutch.

But things are about to alter: I see the rosy fingers of the dawn. They are altering in Washington first of all. This is only proper. As H. L. Mencken revealed, after arduous researches, it was there that the American bathtub was shyly introduced to fame. If President Millard Fillmore left no other monument behind him, he will be remembered for installing the first tub in the White House. It stood six inches above the floor on its iron-claw feet.

The result was the cleanest presidency ever. For even the raunch-iest politicians, like Sockless Jerry Simpson, soap succeeded bear's grease, and America was on its way to becoming the most san-itized of all the empires on the globe.

Yet somehow the bathtub got lost as we careened through the twentieth century. Till now. The present forces behind the revival of the tub have planned well. Appropriately, they are beginning their attack with Washington. Not the Capitol or the White House, however; that would be too obvious. The antitub legions would demand a congressional hearing; there would be impassioned pleas for tax-supported scruffiness. Redolent pickets would march back and forth holding signs such as MAKE PEACE NOT TUBS or DON'T UP THE TUB.

So the outpost of the tub is ten miles from the White House, in the plushy suburb of Bethesda, which the leaders of the move-ment have picked for its biblical associations. They have out-fitted a showroom under the suggestive title of "Baths Interna-tional." What they have there would make your blue eyes pop.

Bathroom after bathroom—and all so elegant that you could stand for more than a minute, jaw slack, without knowing what they were for. Gone is the black and white tile; in its place lush carpeting wall to wall, mauve or magenta, purple or puce. Gone are the cheap chrome fixtures; in their place gold of course, platinum, and, for those of us who love inverse snobbery, pewter. What distinguishes the toilets is that not one looks like a toilet. But the bathtubs we recognize, after the initial tingle of surprise, for what they are.

But what a difference there is, for these carry our fantasies far beyond De Mille. Did you ever dream of a His and Hers bathtub set? I quote faithfully from the brochure which Baths Interna-tional is trying to slip into the *Congressional Record*: "Lady's Bath features a sunken tub surrounded by a moat (stocked with gold-fish), a smoked mirror wall and ledge for planting." Across the aisle we can stare enviously at the "Man's Bath which could easily double as a study. Background combines paneled walls with bronze articulations, bronze paper ceiling, and a fireplace." Man, think of it, bronze articulations—and a fireplace!

Do you yearn for a touch of the Orient? You can get a "Japanese Soaking Tub in lacquer red, reached by teak slatted steps."

Would you wish your tub covered over with a laminated fabric of roses or daffodils or daisies? You can get it. Would you like it in dimpled leather panels instead? It's yours.

I've saved the best for the last. It's a heart-shaped tub for two, in apricot and lustrous black. At the top of the heart an upholstered bolster invites you and your companion to rest your head in comfort while you soak. You switch on the luscious, if canned, music; you switch off the overhead reading lamps; and you drowse with your companion while the rough world drops away.

Pretty sybaritic, but it's coming. Which one would I pick? I don't really know. After all, though Mencken was the prime historian of the American tub, he himself shunned it and took a shower instead—ice-cold—every morning.

51

Caverns for the Cavemen

A man's club makes a potent appeal to two of his deepest though least fashionable urges. One is to gather with a few of his fellows and shut out the rest. The other is to tolerate women in the club only as servants or guests.

As I observe such clubs currently, I must conclude that they'll either bend or break. Or, to put it more precisely, they'll either accommodate or wither. Meanwhile, I suggest that they're worth a look—for the same reason that we gaze with mild interest at other survivals from the prehistoric past, the sluggish iguana, say, or the flittering bat.

The men's clubs of London remain the most renowned of their kind. Alike in still being citadels of male independence, they otherwise vary richly from one another. The first time I lunched at the Athenaeum I actually glimpsed a bishop in gaiters; the first time I lunched at the Savage Club a member was wearing his necktie for a belt and doing a few steps of hornpipe as he bounced by our table.

Each club there has its own atmosphere. A few have a stuffiness which nearly stifles; you feel that you're in a smog alert. But most merely have a pleasantly individual air, for example, the Garrick with its handsome stage setting for the apostles of the arts who make up much of the membership. The great actor David Garrick examines us from his portrait with a quizzical gaze as we mount the marble staircase.

But let's come closer to home. The men's clubs of Washington pale before their full-blooded English peers. Yet they have a life of their own and, even on a cursory inspection, some significant tribal differences. Four of the most prominent are—and in an excess of tact I list them alphabetically—the Army and Navy Club, the Cosmos Club, the Metropolitan Club, and the National Press Club. Recently, imitating the modes of the social scientists, I decided to do a brief study of them. I prayerfully compiled a set of questions, each question quite different from the others, with help from my pocket computer.

How good is the food? How do the members greet one another in the washroom? How large is the library? How helpful is the switchboard? The answers to those queries turned out, as I had hoped, to throw a shaft of light on the nature of the four clubs.

As a matter of fact, the reception at the switchboard should come first because I got some of my data by phone. But not all, for I'm a card-carrying member of the Cosmos Club, have lunched at the other three, and enjoy full access to native informants.

Highest marks for helpfulness go to the ladies at the switchboard of the Army and Navy Club; the lowest go to the Metropolitan Club, where the urge to bar the rest of the world showed a trace of paranoia. The more so since I didn't want to ask how many Blacks belonged or whether a portrait of Ronald Reagan hung on the west wall of the lounge. All I wished to find out on the phone, from the Metropolitan and its brother societies, was the number of books in the library and the menu for, say, that Thursday. Anyhow, the results were enlightening at each of the clubs not only in what was said but how.

The National Press Club is the largest and glossiest of the four, with a staff of over 100. Its telephone tone is hearty and open. Yet its manager required a request in writing before he would agree to mail me a copy of the menu or of the club's news-sheet, the *Record*, which otherwise goes out by the thousands. The club

155

lacks a library in the normal sense of the word, according to the manager, but it owns news tickers and reference books in abundance.

As I intimated, the chilliest club is the Metropolitan. When I asked its manager for the Thursday menu he promised only to think about it. When I asked about the library, he referred me to the part-time librarian but the switchboard had trouble in identifying him and found it impossible to locate him. At the Army and Navy clubs throughout the world, the tradition is to have a modest library tended by the salad chef in his off hours. Not so in Washington, at the home office. A retired colonel has charge of the library here. He assured me without an instant's hesitation that it had 10,000 volumes. The number looked so round and lovely that I confess to a bit of suspicion about its correctness. The Cosmos Club owns a formidable library, in good part through gifts by author-members. They run from such a bestseller as Herman Wouk's *The Winds of War* to such splendidly specialized tomes as *Important Karst Regions of the Northern Hemisphere*, edited by M. Herak and V. P. Springfield. This library too is reported to have about 10,000 volumes, and that I believe.

Competition about the quality of the food is fierce, I find from my native informants. The members of each club avow that theirs is the worst. However, my determination is that the Army and Navy Club serves the tastiest meals; and loyalty keeps me from naming the club which serves the dullest.

The mores of the men's room? My informants agree. Members of the Press Club, on meeting there, greet one another with a jape. The members of the Army and Navy Club exchange a brisk word while zipping up. The members of the Cosmos Club vary in their practice. And the members of the Metropolitan do not speak but bow slightly.

These clubs are all well housed, with the Cosmos occupying the handsomest quarters. All give a feeling of upholstered permanence. But the squalls and storms of change are beating around them. Old members are dying, as old members do, and younger ones are proving hard to recruit. The Press Club now admits women members; the Army and Navy now declines to bar them (there's a working difference). But the Metropolitan and the Cosmos keep out the female sex. It happens that at the Cosmos I myself have twice petitioned for the admission of female members, without avail. Still, the clubs have a sentimental value and I hope they stay. What if, sitting in their leather armchairs, the members look a little stuffed?

52

A Few Clichés for a
Counter-Commencement

We march in, blackbirds all, except for an occasional bluebird or scarlet tanager, to Elgar's "Pomp and Circumstance, IV." I suspect that the corny old tune still holds some magic for faculty and students alike. I scan the graduates as we pass by them; even with all that hair they look beautiful. Young, fresh, open.

Seated, I settle back with my faculty colleagues and wait philosophically for the commencement address. I'm going to play my usual game of counting the clichés as they come reverberating from the loudspeakers. Over the years the average has been gratifying high. Except two years ago, when the speaker looked ready to pop behind the podium if some militant hurled a dead egg. And last year, for that matter, when the president of Hopkins State, glossy with success, urged the advantages of failure. This year we have an eminent newscaster. My own nomination for commencement speaker was Shirley Chisholm but you can guess how far that got.

Anyway, Howard K. Kronkite rises with a flurry of robes and speaks in bell-bottle tones for at least three minutes before modestly mentioning Watergate. There turns out to be nothing I can disagree with in what he says. But he says it so unctuously that I feel as I felt when watching that Center-Stage play about the Berrigans: how easy it is to make virtue repellent! So I concentrate on counting the clichés.

Near the end I dream a bit about the address, the counter-commencement address, I'll never hear. The one which will give the kids something for their money. The one which will say something like this:

"Now listen. I want to make a single suggestion. The day after you get home, go over and get yourself a library card. Hurry!

"I have my reasons. Right now you're as friendly to new ideas and unfledged notions as you ever will be. You've been surrounded by change and you've helped create it. I've been watching the alterations in your culture. I note with professional interest that you've deserted handkerchiefs for kleenex, smoothness for hair. You've abandoned loquaciousness for shrugs or gestures, exactness for intimations. You've showed an acceptance of all sorts of sex, including several sorts your parents didn't think existed.

"You've practically bathed in change. But it would be sniveling for me to flatter you by saying that the change has been all to the good. It hasn't. I find, for instance, that you've grown hostile to free speech, that you want to shut off certain ideas only because you find them detestable. You don't all go as far as SDS in driving out race theorists like Jensen and Shockley, but I doubt if you'll agree with me that all ideas should be aired. I find, further, that you're even surer than earlier college generations that you're right. And that the rest of us are wrong.

"Also I feel that—though I can't prove it—you're even surer that you're interesting. So you're prompt to blast some professors for being dull. Have you ever entertained the notion that some students might be dull too? There are some of you sitting here waiting to graduate who, I swear, are interesting only to your mother. A professor can hardly see you without falling asleep.

"But not most of you. I like to believe that most of you are both brighter and brisker than your parents. The problem, educationally, is to keep you that way. That's why I push the library card. Your parents' notions are perhaps twenty-five years old, notions they got when they were your age. The best way, almost the only way, to keep your own stock of ideas fresh and flexible is through reading. Reading books.

"I'm sorry but no other way comes close. Television? The news you watch is little but headlines. The documentaries are so random that you can't count on them. Newspapers? Right now they look fine. But the press in general is a survey and a supplement, an entertainment more than an instruction. Then too, the press is congenitally inaccurate. In every news story I've known firsthand, there's been a touch of either carelessness or bias. Of course I'm guilty of it myself. The Washington *Post*, now riding high, is a noteworthy example of bias. It's consistently effusive toward poor Blacks and condescending to poor whites.

"The movies? Once again, entertainment not instruction, and nowadays kinky entertainment at that. Everything they touch becomes more garish, the sex weirder, the violence more degenerate. To take just one example: compare the original story with the film version of *Cabaret*. You come away from the movie feeling smeared.

"The general magazines? They're either dying or already dead. What's left is the specialized and professional magazines. They're good but they're not enough. You still need books.

"So get that card and go to the library once a week. Simplistic though it sounds, I'm convinced that it's the best way to stay educated. If you keep abreast of ideas, then you may help us all to survive. You may even have a chance to see Thoreau's promise at the end of *Walden* realized: 'There is more day to dawn. The sun is but a morning star.' Who knows?

"By the way, don't you think for a moment that I can't recognize what that young fellow, with his clipboard and pencil, is doing in the corner. He's counting the clichés!"

53

Ginger Snaps

Must reform always look at us lugubriously down its blue nose? I wouldn't think so. Wit and satire can be effective reformers too. Remember the gallows-humor of the antismoking commercials on television? I think of them every time I see a newspaper ad featuring some cowboy puffing contentedly in Marlboro Country—I expect him to break up in fits of hacking. Women's liberation likewise has its gallows-humor but I find it a more frantic kind, though less in the magazine *Ms* perhaps than in the manifestoes and flyers. Anyhow, I suggest that Women's Liberation might reach back and take a leaf from Fanny Fern.

Fanny Fern was the wittiest women's-rights propagandist we had in, I claim, the whole nineteenth century. Most of the women's-rights pioneers looked as if they were sitting in a cold bathtub. Not Fanny. She was as sprightly as the "Ginger Snaps" she specialized in. These were metaphorical rather than literal—tart little essays defending women and scolding men. They became enormously popular though completely forgotten today. "Fanny Fern" was the pen name picked by Sara Payson Willis Parton and of course it sounds ridiculous to us. But her writing keeps the buoyancy of youth.

She briskly describes herself, at her peak it happens, in *Folly as It Flies*: "Heavens! I am fifty-five, and feel half the time as if

161

I were just made. . . . I like a nice bit of beefsteak and a glass of ale, and anybody else who wants it may eat pap. I go to bed at ten and get up at six. I dash out in the rain, because it feels good on my face. I don't care for my clothes, but I *will* be well; and after I'm buried, I warn you, don't let any fresh air or sunlight down on my coffin, if you don't want me to get up."

That was Fanny. She had two chief targets: man, the pompous unfeeling male, and the female who announces that " 'Woman's Rights' simply sets her to giggling." Fanny also detested the female who pouts that such rights would make her less feminine. It gives you a sense of the passing of time to realize what the charge was a century ago against the franchise. "As to the principal objection urged against voting," Fanny must write, "I think a woman may vote, and yet be a refined, and lady-like, and intelligent person."

The readers she wrote for were middle-class women and the more understanding among their husbands. In *Ginger-Snaps*, and other volumes of her collected periodical pieces, she turns her wry wit in manifold directions. Though she can take the long view, she generally likes to write about nearby things. In "Blue Monday" it's the weekly washing. In "The Old Maid of the Period" it's the besotted male notions about the maiden lady. In "Men and Their Clothes" it's the male peacock who proudly dresses himself as a crow. Fanny jeers at the stovepipe hat, the swallowtail coat, and the stiff shirt-collar, whether it "stands up like a picket on guard, or lays over, with a necktie to tie it suffocatingly over the jugular vein."

But she becomes barbed when she thinks about the two classes of women for whom, in her day, life proved especially dreary. One was the farm wife, now disappearing from our culture. Fanny catalogs her duties: raising children and chickens; making butter, cheese, bread, and the eternal American pie; sewing clothes for her whole household and then washing those clothes, eternally thereafter; minding the barnyard and the garden; tending the children through all the children's diseases of that era— all this "besides keeping a perpetual river of hot grease on the kitchen table, in which is to float potatoes, carrots, onions, and turnips for the ravenous maws of the 'farm-hands.' " No wonder

162

she ends as nothing but a drudge. Her husband, in contrast, has an easy time; he is simply a "round, stalwart, comfortable animal."

The other class of women are the working girls in a big city. In "The Working-Girls of New York" Fanny describes their state with a telling combination of wit and rage. She paints a picture of their day. It begins at dawn in a tenement where they share a cubbyhole and bed with another girl. They pull on their sleazy, tawdry clothing and then hurry to the factory where they work. The factory Fanny describes makes hoopskirts on machinery which clatters every minute. The girls start up the machines at seven in the morning and stay at them till six at night, with half an hour off at noon for a slice of bread and butter. This is their existence, week after week, month after month. Who can blame the few pretty ones if they try easier ways of making money? "Talk of virtue!" Fanny hoots.

The only hope, Fanny says, lies in the newly formed "Working Woman's Protective Union" and it can't do much. However, she cheers it on.

Most of the time she deals with subjects somewhat less grim, such as her delightful "Washing the Baby"; and her touch is usually light. Still, she knows what she is doing and she once remarks that her subjects are more profound than funny. It's a stimulating experience to read her today, to see what has remained unchanged in American life and what has altered. *Ginger-Snaps* appeared over a century ago, and for me it reads fine. I can't help wondering how *Vaginal Politics*, say, will read when it's over a century old. Of this I'm sure: the position of women will be as different in the 2070s as it is now when compared with Fanny's day. Peering into my foggy crystal ball, I predict entire sexual equality accompanied by the withering of the family and the rearing of the children in local kibbutzes.

54

Raping Clio Right and Left

In my neighborhood I'm noted as the heartiest Anglophile since Benedict Arnold. I'm convinced that the United States and Great Britain must, repeat must, remain not merely allies but friends. My knowledge of foreign policy is as rudimentary as a Texas ambassador's, yet my instincts assure me that no other nation can be as close to ours. Though we may make arrangements with other countries flattering to our national interests, the arrangements are bound to be uneasy ones. How could we ever be comfortable with, say, the Russians or the French?

However, even with Great Britain it isn't easy. The cultural differences between our two nations remain disconcertingly large. They result all too often in an Englishman's thinking that an American is trying to act like him and doing a ludicrous job of it. Or an American's thinking that an Englishman somehow has never really learned to talk English. Not long after I came home from my latest stay to London, I turned once again to a delightful and devastating book which tells us a good deal about the difficulties. It's entitled *The Historian's Contribution to Anglo-American Misunderstanding*. It was prepared by a binational posse of historians, headed by Ray Billington of the Huntington Library in California, a former Harmsworth Professor at Oxford.